D1086530

## KNOW YOUR DREAMS

Have you ever dreamed of standing outside a cathedral? Or a church? This is nearly always an indication that luck is coming your way.

## KNOW YOUR DICE

Roll a five and you can expect to meet a new person who should prove to be a great friend.

## KNOW YOUR STARS

Born between July 22 and August 21? You are capable of feeling very deeply for others and are extremely sympathetic.

## KNOW YOUR FUTURE

through any of the dozen fascinating "inside" yet classic ways described and detailed by the master Futurecaster himself, Maurice Woodruff. The results are virtually guaranteed to be astounding!

## Other SIGNET Titles of Special Interest

# *The Secrets*

of

# FORETELLING YOUR OWN FUTURE

*by*

*Maurice Woodruff*

A SIGNET BOOK from
**NEW AMERICAN LIBRARY**
TIMES MIRROR

COPYRIGHT © 1969 BY MAURICE WOODRUFF

*All rights reserved*

SIXTH PRINTING

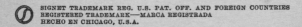
SIGNET, SIGNET CLASSICS, SIGNETTE, MENTOR AND PLUME BOOKS
*are published by The New American Library, Inc.,*
*1301 Avenue of the Americas, New York, New York 10019*

FIRST PRINTING, MAY, 1969

PRINTED IN THE UNITED STATES OF AMERICA

# CONTENTS

Foreword     vii

    I.   Astrology     11

   II.   Telepathy     42

  III.   The Analysis of Dreams     45

  IV.   Phrenology     98

   V.   Foretelling the Future by Dice     102

  VI.   Napoleon's Prediction Spinner     106

 VII.   Cartomancy: A Guide to Reading Cards     114

VIII.   Numerology     118

  IX.   Palmistry     121

   X.   Handwriting     130

  XI.   Superstitions     138

 XII.   Fun—and the Future—in a Teacup     149

# ★ Foreword ★

When one thinks of foretelling the future, one immediately calls to mind the word destiny; this word has often been, and still is, given a wrong slant because a lot of people mention it with a feeling of reproach and others argue that it just cannot be. The mistake occurs because these people do not look for the true meaning of the word; it derives from the word destination—in other words, a goal, which is aimed at by each individual of his own free will.

Quite often, someone may say to me, "Oh, this is quite silly, because if it is my destiny to do something, then it will happen anyhow"—which is not quite true, because if this were the case, my work, and that of many others, would not be as useful as it has proven to be. The art of foretelling the future falls much more under the heading of guidance. It is my opinion that the only occurrences that are predestined are birth and death. Nearly everything that happens to us in life, other than these two events, has a two-way prong; therefore, it is the job of a man who is looking into the future to say, "This is going to happen. It can either happen in one way or another—if you want my advice, you will approach it *this* way, because this will make it easier for you."

Another point that many maintain is that those who foretell the future must have a terrific influence over the people for whom they are forecasting; again this is erroneous, because, first, as I have said, everybody possesses free will, and second, to be able to forecast the future with sincerity and validity, one must be, to a certain point, a psychologist—enough of one to know whether or not your sitter can take the bad news as well as the good. Remember that nothing happens to anybody in this life that is so bad (apart from death) that a compensation does not eventually follow—in other words, you could even have several terrible days, but eventually one will bring a happy compensation. Thus, when foretelling the future, one should be honest enough to say that these things are going to happen, but do not worry, because this happy event will follow, and thus psychologically the sitter will be able to accept the bad in order to reach the good. Also, a rounding out must apply. You do not just tell a person that he is going to move. You say why, and, also, when your gift has advanced enough, you say to what area and for what reason.

A lot of damage has been done over the years by charlatans in this work, who thought that they could be one step ahead of others by foretelling the future; they have played on the gullibility of their sitters, and I am the first to condemn such people. I believe quite firmly that everybody is psychic. It is a gift that has fallen into disuse. Women might call it intuition. Men perhaps say that they have had a "hunch." How many times have you said, "I knew darn well that that was going to happen," but you didn't know why? This in itself is a proof of the existence of prophetic ability. Some might say that you are able to foretell the future by grouping people according to their general appearance or behavior. This again is not correct, for life is not a circus where you take human beings and train them to do their best tricks; we are at all times striving for self-understanding and knowledge. The world now has become a nerve center. People are more educated and want to know the why's and wherefore's, and there is a much greater feeling of insecurity than at any time before.

I have written this book, in layman's language, because I am so often asked how does one do this work. I shall try to give you a simple look at the different ways there are of foretelling the future; there are many more ways than those I shall write about, but the ones I include I feel are the outstanding methods. My hope is that when you have read each chapter you will have a more adequate feeling of both your own characteristics and your standard of being able to judge others. To be able to foretell the future, one of the most important qualities is sympathy for your fellow human being; by sympathy, I mean a greater knowledge of what goes into making a person tick, and the realization that we all have human frailties (the perfect person has not yet been born—each and every one of us necessarily needs guidance). Remember that if you want to describe a sunrise, it is a most difficult thing to do in words. You have to see the sunrise with your own eyes. Each of you will read the following chapters with certain differences of opinion; if you want to learn from them, you will form your own mental images.

# Chapter I

## ★ ASTROLOGY ★

Long before the words "clairvoyance," "extrasensory perception," "precognition" and the like became an accepted part of our everyday language, man was seeking to know himself and to discover ways and means of looking into the future. It all started—probably in the third millennium B.C.—with the study of the stars. Over the centuries this effort to know the future has grown in many ways, so that now man seeks guidance not only from the heavens but from many other sources as well.

Astrology has been hailed, however, as "the supreme science." It has also been rejected as an invention of the devil. It has been the object of ridicule, mockery, attack and mass hysteria. Alternately, it has been both acknowledged by the church and reviled.

But astrology has survived. Today the early primitive study of the stars has developed into far wider fields of scientific research which cover medical astrology, mathematical astrology, biological astrology and weather astrology.

Here are just a few of the advantages that a proper understanding of astrology can give:

1. It provides a key to character and personality so that you may develop all that is best in you and control and minimize all that is negative. ("You can take precautions against your own tempera-

11

ment just as you can against bad weather"—
Claudius Ptolemy, second century A.D.)
2. It imparts understanding of the feelings and temptations of others.
3. It gives foreknowledge of the dangers to which, by reason of the moment of your birth, you may be predisposed, thus enabling you to take arms against them.
4. It makes you aware of potential talents and abilities so that you may develop these and make the fullest use of them to ensure a happier, fuller, richer life.
5. It enables you to recognize the moment when that tide which "taken at its flood leads on to fortune" comes your way.
6. It foretells the possibilities of the future so that when fortunate times are with you, you are ready to take full advantage of them, and, when aspects are not as good, you can save yourself, by self-restraint, from both heartache and hardship.

## ARIES—March 21st to April 20th

Aries is the first sign of the Zodiac and the strongest of all the signs. Its subjects are very true to the symbol of their sign (a ram possessing rather formidable horns).

People who are born during this period always want to be right at the head of whatever they set out to do, for they are rulers and pioneers. As they are only happily satisfied when things are going as they intend and want them to be, they do, in consequence, quite often fail as employees. Their ideas are dogmatic to the point of self-righteousness, yet they are more often than not proved right in the long run.

Because they possess the ability to see just what lies ahead of them, they know how to plan for what is most likely to happen. It is much better for these people to be able to give orders and directions rather than to have to take them from others, for while they are capable of leading in a strangely accomplished manner, they cannot at all times be relied on to do a job competently themselves. If ever a sign may be said to indicate a "jack of all trades," then it is Aries.

Arians are extremely fond of travel, and they usually get around to doing a great deal of it. They are very fond of change, too, and never seem to want to stay put in any one situation or place.

Taken all round, these people are very headstrong, enthusiastic, and impulsive; sometimes they are self-willed to the point of annoyance, especially when they feel that they are on to a good thing. If you want to see all discretion thrown to the wind, and feel the lash of their tongue, cross them—and I can assure you that you will certainly get your wish.

However, it would be difficult to find yourself a better friend in this world than an Arian subject, for they can be extremely gentle as well as outspokenly frank. It is one of their very well-known faults to be at times almost stupidly overgenerous—to the point of embarrassment.

Arians born in March often possess extremely quick tempers which can be quite uncontrollable at times. They are impulsive. Those born between April 1st and 10th are clever; they may appear to give way, yet get just what they want all the same. They are affectionate, faithful people.

Those born between April 11th and 20th are the ones who most closely resemble their birth sign, the Ram. They will rush into anything without any sign of fear, and you may be certain that should you at any time upset anyone to whom they are particularly attached—then heaven help you. This type will get the world for you at one moment, and want to murder you the next.

Most Arians have two distinct sides to their character. The first indicates a rather cocksure and overconfident nature which, while being strongly sensitive, is much inclined to jealousy and the dogmatic. The other side is very ambitious and appreciative of even the tiniest thing which may be done to help them; this side possesses a strongly developed desire to help weaker people.

Constitutionally, the Arian is lucky, for he has a strong

resistance to infection and disease. Headaches and sinus conditions can affect Arians however, as can strain and overwork. On the whole, they have long lives, but nearly always have to take to wearing glasses as the years go by.

From experience, I have learned that the "luck-bringers" for those born under this sign are likely to be as follows:

Their colors are without doubt all shades of scarlet and pillar-box red.

The jewel for them to wear—and peculiarly enough they nearly always do—is the diamond.

The day of the week which is likely to prove the most propitious for them is usually a Tuesday or a Thursday.

The month (or months) most likely to be favorable to them cannot be singled out, for in the case of Arians during the coming year, for instance, good fortune is quite evenly distributed throughout, with possibly a slight inclination toward the autumn months.

One interesting point however: In the main, Arians should try to avoid tying up with a Scorpion in business or even socially.

Marriage partners for them are best selected from the Leo group (July 22nd to August 21st) or from Gemini (May 21st to June 20th).

Should their selection prove to be a Leo type, then they may expect this person to be most agreeable, yet at the same time very self-controlled. Tact will be needed at times, for there will be moments when it will be difficult to know just what has angered the Leo subject, who may be apt to take action without warning and allow feelings to overrule caution. These people can, however, be extremely sympathetic.

On the other hand, should the selection be a Gemini subject, the Arian will have for a mate an intellectual who will live more in the mind and will not be ruled by feelings which need to be overcome. Gemini subjects suit an Arian well, for they also hate to be stuck in one place for too long at a time and like constant change. Never try to make them complete one thing before starting on another, though, for this is something they rarely do. If you want to influence them to do something your way, then try to point out very clearly just what you feel should be done —and in this way avoid what could prove to be a most irritating obstinacy.

## TAURUS—April 21st to May 20th

Taurus is the second sign of the Zodiac. This is a very fixed sign and its subjects are usually practical and solid types. They can be most reserved when the occasion merits it and can also be most determinedly stubborn.

Patience, reliability and honesty are their greatest assets, and because of these qualities they more often than not hold down executive positions very capably. When roused, they have very quick and sharp minds and tongues. Before anyone tries to fool a Taurian subject, he should make certain he knows what he is up against, for you can take a Taurian just so far and absolutely no farther.

Taurians do not waste either their emotions or their energies. They hide their emotions well, although, if they are driven too far, they see red. They should not be provoked, otherwise you may find yourself face to face with a person who may well resemble a maddened bull.

Taurians are often extremely impressed by outstanding experiences, and through the thoughts and feelings that result from them they can very often be described as psychic types. When they concentrate in this field, they can invariably be relied on to be very near the mark.

The mate who tries to deceive a Taurian partner does not hold a very good hand, for quite often Taurians will surprise even themselves by a statement about either the past or the future "out of the blue," with no previous knowledge, which will turn out to be absolutely accurate. They are gifted with the strongest of intuition and this, I feel, stems from the fact that they are naturally fatalists, which, in turn, helps them to control their emotions.

Where finances are concerned, it is unusual for Taurians to be able to steer a middle course. They either make a great deal of money or they make nothing worthy of mention. They may be stubborn or lazy, or, in complete contrast, unselfish, generous and at times even overenergetic.

Again, we have three types born under this sign. Those born during the latter days of April tend to be the stubborn ones. You nearly always have to go to some pains to persuade them to make a change, say. They can be lazy, too.

Those whose birthday falls between May 1st and 10th are the ones who make first-class buyers because of their excellent powers of discrimination. They are thrifty and can, in consequence, often be thought of as mean, yet would be shocked to be told so.

And there are those born between May 11th and 20th who are apt to be very generous and exceptionally genuine types. These are the ones who will do anything within reason for you without any thought of return. They have wills of iron and it is rare to hear of a failure in this group. At the same time they are not the easiest people in the world to work for, for they demand, and insist on getting, perfection.

From experience, it has been found that the Taurian group produces really excellent buyers (men and women), doctors, fashion stylists and bankers. They also do well in any other trade or profession that demands a high standard of practical ability plus strong determination. They are not particularly quick in financial matters but it is difficult to fool them in this field.

Constitution-wise, Taurians are lucky, inasmuch as they usually have good health. Heart conditions may trouble them a little in later life. Their weakest points are their throats and kidneys. Fortunately, their naturally strong constitutions normally enable them to control their weaknesses and they are not likely to overindulge themselves or live unwisely.

"Luck-bringers" for Taurians are as follows:

The colors best suited to them are blues, in any shade. The jewel they should wear whenever possible is the emerald, although from experience I have learned that quite often the ruby has the same effect.

The day of the week which I find is likely to be best suited for important developments may be either a Monday or a Friday.

The month most likely to produce outstanding events for them is October, in the near future, at any rate.

Marriage partners for them are ideally selected from subjects of Virgo (August 22nd to September 21st) or Capricorn (December 21st to January 19th).

Should the choice be from among the subjects of Virgo, then they can expect their partner to be very methodical and at times rather critical, one who does not waste time on dreaming, is very intelligent, a little difficult to convince at times, the "cool" type who will always have one eye open for the "main chance." It is much better to leave this type alone should they show the desire to argue, for the chances are that, in this way, they will come round to your point of view quite quickly.

However, should the choice be from among the subjects of Capricorn, a Taurian can expect his partner to be someone who will really enjoy the feeling that he or she is helping to build up his spouse to some high position. There will be no bounds to the Capricornian ambition in this direction. The Capricornian may at times be irritating because of a tendency to be painstakingly slow and cautious. There can also be a lack of demonstration of affection.

## GEMINI—May 21st to June 20th

Gemini is the third sign of the Zodiac. It is an impressionable sign and belongs to people who are usually very intelligent. Their ambitions increase their desire for knowledge. At times they are apt to be far too critical and analytical.

They are just the reverse of idealists, and it would be hard to find a more materialistic type. At times they can be most annoying because of their stubborn skepticism; they nearly always want to push ahead with some new job before they have completed the one at hand. Changes and moves come as second nature to them, and they find it very trying to have to stay in one place for any length of time.

Because of this love of change, Gemini subjects do at times get the reputation of being rather unreliable, but they are not. The constant urge for change is more often than not a strong cause for indecision in them. Faced with two alternatives, they frequently become restless and nervous. Then they start to fret and may become very stubborn indeed and at the same time irritable and snappy.

One can never accuse them of being too expressive orally in anything to do with the emotions. They prefer to show their feelings in actions rather than words.

Once they get an idea firmly in mind, they can be most determined. They often meet up with success as editors, teachers or secretaries—and because they are always gluttons for work, they may make extra money by doing more than one task at a time.

If you are dealing with Gemini subjects, you may find it hard to convince them of your point of view; they like absolute proof of ultimate success before taking on anything new. At the same time, they are very quick-witted, often quite clever and trigger-sharp in repartée, with a fair degree of subtlety.

Of the three different types under Gemini, the first are those born between May 21st and May 31st. These are almost always true to the sign, and sometimes unable to concentrate with any great degree of success because of their state of flux.

Those born between June 1st and 10th are the ones who make good headway in life because, being critical, they are usually the most balanced subjects of the sign.

Those born between June 11th and 20th are the humanitarians of the sign, fond of children, animals and people. They are the kindly, sociable ones, loyal to an extreme degrce. They rarely show their hurts or heartbreaks outwardly and are very nice people.

Constitutionally, subjects of Gemini do not always have great strength. They suffer from nervous exhaustion owing to their inclination to worry over minute details. Bronchitis and rheumatism are not unknown to them, yet it is a fact that if they do take extra care when quite young, they will avoid many discomforts at a later age.

"Luck-bringers" for them are as follows:

The colors that seem to help them to prosper are yellow and orange, and, sometimes, all shades of green.

The jewel to be worn when possible is the agate, but it has been found that gold worn on its own has the same effect.

The day of the week strongly indicated for good fortune may be either Sunday or Thursday, sometimes both.

The month of the year for them is April, but they would do well to take caution during February.

Marriage: In the choice of a partner, they would do well to bear in mind that they link up extremely well with either a Libra subject (born between September 22nd and October 22nd) or with an Aquarian (born January 21st to February 18th). A Capricorn subject is seldom a successful marriage partner for them.

If their choice should fall on a Libran, then they may expect their partner to be sensitive and very fair-minded, a family type who is both artistic and fond of pleasure, one who can be quite easily hurt but who is most thoughtful of others.

On the other hand, should they choose to tie up with an Aquarian, here they will find the quiet, inoffensive person who may at times be rather difficult for the Gemini subject to understand. Try to bear in mind in this instance that it is the refined side of life that appeals most to an Aquarian; never ridicule his ideas or thought for others, and, above all else, be completely honest with him or he may go off without a word—and not listen later to explanations, either.

## CANCER—June 21st to July 21st

Cancer is the fourth sign of the Zodiac and is well known for producing those who are the strongest maternal types.

Its subjects are usually brimming over with feeling. They are generous, very sensitive and mostly inclined to be rather retiring. Their characteristics are unlike those of others born under any other sign, and absolutely peculiar to them. On one hand, they are full of rather attractive little idiosyncrasies; on the other, they are absolute sticklers for convention.

At all times they like to be noticed and, although they do put up the facade of an unassuming attitude, it is never terribly difficult to bring a Cancer subject forward.

Thrifty they most certainly are when they want to be, and the wonderful gift of imagination which they possess immediately places them in the romantic class. Once angered, they can be most contrary. This in turn can lead to extreme irritability and peevishness unless they have their tempers well under control.

One of their greatest faults is indecision, and consequent hesitation. They can at times be extremely exasperating until they have learned to get over this hurdle. Once this is conquered, they will be able to get their own way through willpower and perseverance—and by means of gentle persuasion rather than irritatingly persistent reminders.

Going further into their personalities, it is very often found that these people are tireless and very ambitious, or, on the other hand, sluggish and lazy. All Cancer representatives do have one thing in common, however. That is their love of antiques, old people, old buildings—in fact, anything known to be of great age. They are gifted with extremely acute memories.

As with other signs of the Zodiac, we can divide those born under Cancer into three groups.

Those born between June 21st and 30th are the most sensitive types. When they have an ambition, they can be steadily persistent until it is achieved.

Those born between July 1st and 10th are the most spectacular ones of the sign. Gifted with good looks and a strong physique, they have the gift of possessing a terrific hold on life, and it is difficult not to grant these people their own way because, when they put themselves out, they can be extremely persuasive. Malice is not an unknown factor in their character and they can be rather dangerous if upset, and are inclined to be unforgiving by nature. They are capable of great jealousies too.

The third group under this sign are those born between July 11th and 20th. These are usually the nicest of the Cancer subjects; they are extremely sympathetic and very kindhearted. Normally, they do "see their ship come in," but have to wait until rather late in life for this.

It is a known fact that most Cancer types do extremely well as nurses, managers, caterers and manufacturers. Cancer is a watery sign and all subjects are normally good sailors. Most appear to do very well financially at some stage of life.

Constitutionally, the Cancer subject is not the strongest. The stomach is inclined to give the most bother, especially when there is any worry. Indigestion and rheumatism are not unknown to them and, when under strain at any time, they do appear to give way temporarily rather easily.

The following are my "luck-bringers" for the Cancer subject:

The colors most fortunate for them are green and gray.

The jewel is their birthstone, which is the ruby.

The day of the week most likely to be propitious for them is either a Thursday or a Saturday. Most certainly never a Monday.

The month can be either one of two—April or September.

Marriage: Cancer subjects invariably meet with great success and happiness if they select a partner from either Scorpio (born between October 23rd and November 21st) or Pisces (February 19th to March 20th). It is just as well for them to remember that they are taking a big chance if they decide to tie up with an Arian (born between March 21st to April 20th).

Should the choice be a Scorpio subject, then they can expect to be mated to a rather dogmatic, possessive type of person, who would, if he thought it necessary, cast everybody else out of his life in order to concentrate on his mate, wishing to protect his own at all times, and inclined to be overambitious for anyone who belongs to him. Should your choice fall on one of this sign, try to remember always that there will be times when you will have to choose your words carefully, because, being sensitive like yourself, Scorpions do not forget easily when they are upset and you may well be treated to a session of sulks.

On the other hand, should your choice be for a Pisces subject, then you can expect a really fine marriage, for these people are receptive as well as impressionable. Never expect them to be either very determined or very persistent, yet do remember their emotions. Let them know that you are there to back them up at all times when they are depressed (which is a thing you will find them rather apt to be from time to time). Keeping this in mind, you cannot choose a better mate.

## LEO—July 21st to August 21st

Leo is the fifth sign of the Zodiac. It is rather a fiery sign which is very fixed and the people who are born under it are nearly always determined people, faithful types whose generosity and emotions are sometimes at fault, because they seem to know no bounds whatsoever.

They are capable of feeling very deeply for others and are extremely sympathetic. This helps to make them wonderful listeners, an asset which those born under other signs very seldom possess except through strong determination and personal effort.

Leo subjects can adapt themselves very harmoniously to whatever their circumstances may be, yet they are headstrong when their feelings are aroused and consequently can be both hasty and passionate.

If you have a Leo type for a friend, then you have a friend indeed, for it is extremely difficult for anyone else to persuade them to listen to any adverse talk about you. Faith and trust are two of their very strongest virtues, and absolute proof of any situation must be produced before they will believe any criticism of a friend. On the other hand, should they ever be convinced that their faith has been misplaced, then you may be sure they will feel most deeply about it.

Leos can really be classed as almost the perfectionists of this life; because they aim so very high, they sometimes find that it takes them quite a while to reach the goal they are striving toward.

At times, the Leo subject is so frank and open in his attitude that it can be irritating to others who do not have these attributes. Never could you accuse them of being secretive, for their belief is that all things should be shared among the ones they love.

If they feel that they have been accused of anything falsely or that anyone has wronged them, then they can be very contemptuous, but they are the first to forgive, and the word "malice" is completely unknown to them.

They are the most self-confident people of all, for they usually possess a strong sense of their own importance in life. They always attempt to be practical in their ideas and this in turn is of great assistance to them when they are trying to adapt themselves to any circumstances in which they may find themselves.

Plodders they most certainly are, for they will go ahead —and keep going—until they get to the very top, and it is their strong intuitive feelings which more often than not give them an advantage over others around them.

If you spend much time in the company of a Leo subject, you will find that because he allows his emotions to run more deeply than most, he is prone to depression, and this may overtake him—for no accountable reason—very suddenly indeed at times.

Leo types have been known to make extremely good organizers, public relations officers, doctors and managers. They are apt to accept any occupation which has as its object the bringing of happiness or benefit to others less fortunate than themselves.

Of the three types born under Leo, those born between July 21st and 31st like to mix socially with the greatest number of people. These are the outstandingly faithful ones of the group.

Those born between August 1st and 10th are those with the most self-confidence and the highest ambitions. This is the type who always keeps to the point, and loves to manage others. They are apt to find themselves in hot water at times because they are too outspoken.

Those born between August 11th and 21st are the most affectionate of all Leo subjects. They can be rather impulsive at times, yet they are very generous and kind. Their one fault is that they find it hard to exercise any patience when trying to get to the heart of anything.

One nearly always finds that Leos as a whole are very cosmopolitan in their outlook and attitude.

Constitutionally, the Leo subject is invariably strong and seems to be gifted with the added asset of having more than a fair share of vitality and energy. This gives tremendous powers of recuperation. If anything, it seems to be the small of the back that is likely to give the most trouble, but on the whole, long, healthy lives are indicated.

Outstandingly lucky points for the Leo type to bear in mind are as follows:

The colors that they should have about them are yellow and gold; when they're faced with difficult tasks, it seems that gold should be given preference.

The jewel that in their case is more true to the sign than any other is their birthstone, which is the sapphire.

The day of the week for them is either a Wednesday or a Thursday, but it will be well for them to try to bear in mind that it is unwise for them to attempt an important undertaking on a Monday.

The month that is likely to bring them outstanding happiness in the near future is March.

Marriage: Unlike those born under other signs of the Zodiac, the Leo subject may well find the perfect mate born under any other sign, with the exception of those born under Capricorn (December 21st to January 19th) and those born under Scorpio (October 23rd to November 21st). These rarely make the best of partners for lasting peace or happiness with the Leo subject.

## VIRGO—August 22nd to September 21st

The celestial sign of Virgo is the sixth of the Zodiac. It is a mutable sign and people who are born under it are usually intelligent, very methodical and with highly developed powers of discrimination. They may at times be a little too critical.

Those born under Virgo certainly cannot be called dreamers, for they are so down-to-earth that they beleive in doing everything in the most matter-of-fact manner possible. By this, I would not say that they cannot believe anything they cannot see, because they do, but being one of the strongest of all business type personalities, they rarely have time to do—or even think about—anything but the matter immediately at hand.

They are self-possessed and very cautious people who at all times have an eye on the main chance.

Because they are so well balanced and determined, and like to work in a peaceful fashion, with no make-believe, they are unlike others born under the other eleven signs—inasmuch as there are few (if any) extremes among Virgo subjects.

They can be relied on to be most discreet because they genuinely prefer not to be in the forefront, and they are apt to take on the atmosphere of others around them rather than create an atmosphere of their own.

Where business is concerned, they seem to have an almost psychic flair, and, because of this, they very often find themselves extremely prone to temptation, though, in nine cases out of ten, they manage to resist the temptations that will undoubtedly come their way.

For the Virgo subject, there is no sentiment in business. They are commercially minded and they seem to have a great deal of success as photographers' models, buyers and sellers, chemists and photographers. It is fairly certain that if you wish to employ a Virgo as a salesman or saleswoman, then he will leave you little to worry about, for your goods will not only sell well but will at the same time become extremely well known.

We have three types born under the sign of Virgo.

Those born between August 22nd and the end of the month are not given to acting on impulse. They are shy, yet at times rather fussy and given to premeditation.

Those born between September 1st and 10th are the most thorough types. They are super-sensitive and very highly critical. They reason everything out in a thoughtful and persistent manner, and thus they meet with a great deal of success.

The last group—those born between September 11th and 21st—possess a reserve which leads them to a less active life than the others of their sign. It is those in this last group who may give way to temptation and are inclined to lead more unconventional lives morally, even though they may be quite firm in other respects.

The constitution of the Virgo type is on an average quite a strong one, but they are inclined to worry much more than others born under other signs of the Zodiac, and are much affected by the people around them. Their main problem may be their tendency to put on far too much weight and this can cause them some discomfort. By watching diets, however, this need never become a serious problem.

Marriage: Virgo people always seem to be faced with quite a problem, for, in this, they do have an almost puritanical outlook.

From experience, it has been found that they match extremely well for happiness with those born under Capricorn (December 21st to January 19th) and with those born under Taurus (April 21st to May 20th). Virgo subjects should never, however, for long-term happiness and contentment marry Scorpios (October 23rd to November 21st).

Should they choose to marry a Capricorn subject, then they can expect their partner to be highly ambitious, to be attracted very much by other people's looks and dress, to be privately rather thrifty and very profound in his ideas. While Capricornians are very self-confident, they can at times be rather cruel in their statements; it would appear that they seldom stop to think before speaking.

If, on the other hand, a Virgoan chooses to marry a Taurian, then he can expect to be given a tremendous amount of strength by his marriage partner. At the same time, he will have to put up with a certain amount of stubborn dogmaticalness demonstrated in a most determined manner. He can know that he is not at any time likely to be let down, but that unless he treats his partner with tact in the early hours of the day, he can be faced with a demonstration of rather fierce temperament for a short period.

The colors most propitious to Virgo subjects are all shades of brown, gray and rust; they are nearly always at their best when these colors are around them.

The jewel for them is with very little doubt the sapphire —a beautiful stone.

The day that is likely to prove the most fortunate for them is a Tuesday, but very rarely should they choose to do anything of great importance on a Monday.

The month cannot be singled out, for, with Virgo subjects, their good fortune and happiness are fairly evenly spread, throughout the coming year, for instance.

## LIBRA—September 22nd to October 22nd

Libra is the seventh sign of the Zodiac, a very well-balanced sign belonging to the refined types who are extremely just in their actions and in their outlook. They are harmonious and happy people.

Gifted with strong artistic ability, they are generous but not stupidly so. It is very difficult for others around the Libran to try to fool him because he has an inbred intuition which rarely plays tricks with him.

Librans are a friendly people whom one likes to meet, and they can make extremely good intermediaries, for they are able to see two sides of an argument and give a completely neutral answer by making fair comparisons. If you wish to get the best work from a Libran, then he must be pressed; he will work quite enthusiastically with the right encouragement and drive.

Nobody could ever say that Librans (who are extremely tactful) are not the easiest of people to get along with. Their disposition is somewhat demonstrative, for they attract their full share of affection and want to be in the limelight. Because of their desire for affection they do at times seem to lack just that necessary amount of toughness when it is needed.

They have extremely accurate powers of perception so that they are not easily fooled by deception. Deceit is the one thing they can rarely forgive or forget; and believe me, deceive a Libran and you may have made quite a strong enemy for life. On the other hand, they will face extreme danger for those they really love.

Where business is concerned, it appears to be the artistic fields that give them their greatest successes. They make really good singers, artists, designers and personal secretaries.

Constitutionally, Librans are generally fairly strong and, in fact, they are not prone to any one great sickness at all as long as they keep on moderate and abstemious lines. They do get a few aches and pains, but luckily they are able to throw these off much more speedily than most people.

With a fair amount of accuracy, we can say that Librans generally are lucky, but nevertheless they also have "luck-bringers" which have stood the test of time:

The colors that are most advantageous for them are green, blue and brown (a far wider choice than most other signs give).

The jewel for them is the stone of balance, which is the opal.

The days of the week which usually turn out to be extremely fortunate are Wednesdays and Saturdays, but not, in the usual run, Fridays.

The month for them is August but not September.

Marriage: When it comes to the selection of a mate, they seem always to do extremely well when they marry either an Aquarian type (January 20th to February 18th) or a Gemini type (May 21st to June 20th).

Should their choice be an Aquarian, they may find their partner at times a little difficult to understand, for although Aquarians are patient and humane, they can be too quiet and a little too highly intellectual. They are honest and they mean well but can be capricious and possessive.

On the other hand, should they choose to tie up with a Gemini type, then they must be prepared to accept a certain amount of stubbornness and bear in mind that they do not have the most demonstrative of partners. Even though Gemini subjects are extremely loyal, they instinctively believe more in deeds than in words. They are sensitive and sometimes appear a little unreliable because of their strong state of indecision. Yet they would almost die for anyone they love.

## SCORPIO—October 23rd to November 21st

Scorpio is the eighth sign of the Zodiac. It is a fixed sign and therefore the characters that it produces are likely to be quietly controlled. Personally, they have many attractive qualities; they are firm and yet cohesive. They are extremely discreet and cautious, and must know exactly what makes anything in particular tick before they will go rushing in and commit themselves.

Quite naturally, they like encouragement and praise where work is concerned, but this does not enter into their calculations when they start to tackle any task at hand.

We have two completely opposite camps of Scorpio subjects. There are those who are absolutely determined and positive about getting whatever job they have on hand done competently, and who are discretion personified. They are nice people as long as you do not cross them.

And there are those who are inclined to be selfish, and in consequence become a little crafty. They work only for their own benefit and do not very much care how much they may hurt anyone else on the way just as long as they reach their own objective.

Scorpio types are helped tremendously by their extra-shrewd judgment of people and things. They have more concealed power in them than can be found in those born under other signs. They possess rather intense tempers and are at times, I'm afraid, a little envious and jealous of others; I have yet to meet a Scorpio subject who is not just a little bit suspicious of the actions of others around him.

We can again divide those born under this sign into three groups. First there are those born between October 23rd and 31st. These are the loyal ones who are capable of being influenced by others around them. They have a natural modesty which quite often keeps them contentedly in the background; nobody could ever accuse them of being overtalkative—in fact, there are times when you wonder whether you have been able to get the message through and convey to them what is in your mind.

Those born between November 1st and 10th are the more friendly and chatty ones and therefore a little less tactful, being much more open generally in character. This is the nicest of the Scorpio types, for they will at times be inclined to put a great deal of confidence in their colleagues. As a result, however, they do sometimes suffer from other people's dispositions.

Those born between November 11th and 21st are the cohesive ones. Ambition knows no bounds for them, especially where their domestic and business spheres are concerned. These Scorpio subjects will allow nothing to stand in their way, and strong determination is their greatest attribute.

It has been found from experience that some of the best supervisors, policemen and policewomen, government officials, dentists and electricians are born under this sign.

The constitution of the Scorpio type is quite definitely

of the strongest. It is a rare thing for them to have to give in even when undergoing great strain. One might liken them to a power station; they appear to generate a little extra energy just at the last minute when it is most needed.

If anything, it is rheumatism and allied ailments that affect their health most, and then not until late in life.

The following are my "luck-bringers" for the Scorpio types:

Their colors are dark red and crimson and these should be worn whenever possible, for, more than most other people, Scorpions need these colors to build confidence and determination.

The jewel which they should wear, to bring them both good luck and strength, is the topaz.

The day for them to be working out their important problems is invariably a Wednesday, not at any time a Saturday.

The month that appears to be outstanding for the Scorpio type for both good and evil seems always to be February.

Marriage: To meet up with success in this field, it is well for Scorpio subjects to bear in mind that they mate extremely well with either Cancer types (June 21st to July 21st) or—strange as it may appear—with another Scorpio. Marriage with a Pisces (February 19th to March 20th) is seldom successful over a long term.

Should their choice fall on a Cancer subject, they can expect this person to show all the emotions, although he is, by nature, sensitive and timid. If you want to please a Cancer subject then you must notice him and give him all the attentions. Cancerians love to be brought forward, but never appear to do this by their own efforts. They have good brains, and treated properly, can be extremely generous. They have more noticeable characteristics than any of the other signs, and therefore they stick to convention much more closely.

## SAGITTARIUS—November 22nd to December 20th

Sagittarius is the ninth sign of the Zodiac and a rather susceptible sign which belongs mainly to instinctively happy, optimistic types.

These people usually possess an unusual amount of energy and are loyal and extremely understanding when they want to be. When trying to express themselves freely and clearly, they never meet difficulty—and where romance is concerned, or anything over which they may display their affections, they are more demonstrative than those born under any other sign.

Where freedom of thought and action are concerned, they are most determined. They will face tremendous odds to achieve these two things and can never therefore be called conventionalists.

At times, they possess an uncanny instinct for finding out the weak spot in other people and hammering this in. (This may be fortunate for them on occasion but is unfortunate for their associates.)

They are not deceitful types; it would be difficult to find people who are more open and frank. They have high principles, and are very independent by nature.

Tidiness is most certainly not one of their greatest attributes; this is something for which they have no regard. When engaged in anything of importance to them, they can close their eyes to everything that is going on around them.

If you try to stop someone born under Sagittarius from doing what he has made up his mind to do, you will find he'll become almost militant in his attitude toward you, and, believe me, he is at times quite ready for a good fight.

Here again we find three different groups born under this same sign. Those born between November 22nd and 30th are those who nearly always rebel against controls, are very candid and bluntly outspoken. These are the ones who want to take the watch to pieces in order to find out what makes it tick! They have analytical minds.

Those born between December 1st and 10th are the emotional types who find it very hard to keep a secret. They are the debaters of this sign and therefore the most independent of all Sagittarius subjects. Anything of a philosophical nature captures their mind almost immediately.

Those born between December 11th and 20th are often quite falsely accused of being selfish because of their indifference. It would be fairer to say of them that they are the persevering and therefore the super-determined types. Anger them and you will feel the lash of their tongue. They are naturally witty; remember that this is the type that knows instinctively just where to hit to give the greatest hurt.

When seeking success in the working field, Sagittarians could not do better than to look in the directions of teaching or designing. They make excellent workers in any social field, too, and a Sagittarian can become an outstanding cleric.

Constitutionally, the Sagittarian is invariably quite strong. It is wise for one, however, to ease up in activities, and stop worrying, whenever there are even slight danger signals from trouble in the chest. Catarrh and bronchitis are weaknesses, and as much outdoor exercise as possible is essential to the Sagittarian.

Several things are known as "luck-bringers" to this group; from experience, I find the best of these are as follows:

The colors that prove to be the most fortunate for them are purples and all allied shades.

The jewel to be worn most frequently is the turquoise.

The day for them to bear in mind, if they wish to push an important issue of any kind to success, is Friday. Monday is not a good day for this.

The month of the year cannot be singled out. Sagittarians, with their slightly rebellious natures, are apt to bring important issues to a head at any time throughout the year.

Marriage: On the whole, these people seem to find their greatest happiness and success when they select a partner from either Aries (those born between March 21st and April 20th) or from Libra (September 22nd to October 22nd). When married to a Capricorn type, there is little hope of outstanding success or happiness in this partnership for a Sagittarrian.

Should the Sagittarian's choice be Aries, he must expect at times to live in a slightly explosive atmosphere, for even though he is himself rebellious, the Arian must always be the leader. However, the Arian is a perfect foil for his own independent nature, and as far as protection is concerned, he could not find a better mate.

Should the selection be from the sign of Libra, then a peaceful existence lies ahead, and a wide circle of friends. These Sagittarians can always know that they will be treated fairly by their partners, but it is possible that they may sometimes feel that life is dull because, at all times, the Librans will want to please.

## CAPRICORN—December 21st to January 19th

Capricorn is the tenth sign of the Zodiac. It is a distinguished, yet earthy, sign, and a sign of giving.

Those born under it are usually perfectionists in all they do; they are ambitious and idealistic. Their physical appearance leaves little to be desired, for the women of this sign are often beautiful while the men frequently have Adonis-like good looks.

Saving is one of their strongest points, so much so that quite often they may be accused of being more than thrifty.

When they state their views, they are extremely profound. Do not be fooled by their outward appearance of being modest and shy. This only goes to hide their very strong determination, for once they have made up their minds, their perseverance is terrific and one can only hold admiration for them in this area.

Where work is concerned, they will go to any length to

be really efficient and one can never accuse them of rushing any task that they have on hand. A Capricorn subject is virtually impossible to hurry.

You can never at any time accuse them of being conceited or proud; they think far too much of their own self-preservation, and if anything, are among the most friendly types who prefer to mind their own business rather than meddle in the affairs of others.

There are, however, two opposite types born under Capricorn. The first are those who like to become leaders and guides to others around them; the second, those who like to make rather a show of their jobs (much more than is absolutely necessary) and love to be known as "plodders."

For the sake of being able to define the Capricornians as a whole, I have found it helpful to divide the sign into three groups, and describe these people according to the position of the stars at the date of their births. For example, those who were born between December 21st and 31st can at times be rather fickle, I'm sorry to say. This is because of their aptitude for indecision, and because they are given to having rather grand ideas on too large a scale. Yet too often they lack the perseverance that would enable them to complete their ideas before going on to something new, and thus their fortunes do tend to go up and down somewhat.

Those who are born between January 1st and 10th are, with little doubt, the most obstinate ones of this sign, for if you say that "blue is blue" they will quite often argue that it is "pink." They are plodders in a very certain manner, but unhappily they do not possess all the necessary energy. On the whole, these are the most generally likable of the Capricorn types.

Those born between January 11th and 19th are modest types, invariably gifted with very good brains plus an extremely friendly personality. Nine times out of ten, this type improve their standard of living by their own determination and ambition. The only failing that experience has taught me that they have is that quite often they fail to see the opportunities which lie right under their noses.

Normally, Capricornians have been known to meet success as builders, air hostesses, agricultural workers, engineers and mechanics, and on rare occasions they succeed quite well as consultant bankers.

The constitution of the Capricorn subject is wiry and strong, and the interesting thing is that his health normally improves with age. It is difficult to pinpoint any one real element that seriously bothers him because he seems to go under only when depressed, which he is apt to be quite frequently.

I have, through experience, learned that there are four different items that may be termed "luck-bringers" to the Capricorn subject.

The colors that are thought to be both lucky and happy for them are black and dark brown. On rare occasions, multiple reds appear to go with their nature.

The jewel which they should wear in order to bring them their greatest happiness is the garnet; the ruby will have almost the same effect.

The day of the week that without doubt is usually the very best for them to arrange anything of great importance is a Tuesday. They should generally try to avoid doing anything of this nature on a sunday.

The period that is likely to be the most eventful for them is mid-June to mid-July.

Marriage is the one thing that one can never accuse Capricornians of rushing into, for of all people they are the ones who take the most time to make up their minds. Indecision is a strong fault of theirs. It would, therefore, be well for them to bear in mind that they are best suited to either the Virgo type (born between August 22nd and September 21st) or to another Capricornian. They are likely to meet with very little success indeed if they marry a Leo type (born between July 22nd to August 21st).

If their choice is a Virgo type, they can expect this person to be a most generous-hearted partner, although, at times, given to depression. At other times, there will be great happiness, for a Virgo person is inclined to go up and down rather like a seesaw. When "down," though, they are best left alone and not questioned, for the mood is nearly always short-lived.

If, on the other hand, another Capricornian is selected as the opposite number, then they can both expect to run the gamut—laughter, tears, happiness and disappointments

—and they must be prepared to try their level best to go along with the other person, yet at the same time try, through gentle persuasion, to get some of both of their rather grand and ambitious ideas down to earth. I say "persuasion" merely because the Capricornian is normally very easily hurt, and it is better to try to make him see reason by kindness and sweetness rather than to be in any way dogmatic.

## AQUARIUS—January 20th to February 18th

Aquarius is the eleventh sign of the Zodiac, and those born during this period are usually humane, quiet and sympathetic characters who can, at times, be a little difficult to understand. They incline toward the arts, love music and literature, and are enthusiastic theater-goers. Their intuitions, when they are trying to analyze anything deeply, are much to be relied on, for they are undoubtedly studious and deep-thinking by nature.

Not at any time could one say that they are not energetic, for they are nearly always "on the go." When they have something in mind that they are anxious to accomplish, they can be extremely independent and self-willed and will react rather strongly to anyone who may think he can divert them from their purpose.

One can meet up with Aquarians who are selfish and more than a little unreliable. Again you may meet an Aquarian who is conceited, one who is apt to be almost unbearable in his attitude, but these occasions will be rare, for generally those born under this sign are kind and sympathetic to those around them, like to carry on quietly with their aims, and have a genuine ambition to rise above the lower elements that may surround them.

Aquarians put anyone they love on a very high level.

As before, I would like to divide the people of the sign into three groups. Those born between January 20th and 31st are at all times those most suited to make the widest use of their high intelligence; they are alert to the small—as well as the large—events happening around them, and they are so self-disciplined that kindness and courtesy are inherent parts of their nature. These are the natural students of the world.

Those born between February 1st and 10th may well be just the opposite, for obedience is certainly not one of their assets, and because of this they quite often find they suffer disappointments. They are suspicious, find it difficult to trust others, and therefore may miss opportunities which may lie right under their noses. This type does not give either his heart—or his help—to others easily.

In contrast, those born between February 11th and 18th are quite definitely the ones who can get right into the heart of most people and things. They are always worth knowing. Of all the Aquarians, they are the most artistic; one could go so far as to say that they are the people born to the arts. Whatever they do, they do from the heart and with great concentration.

Most Aquarians, however, have one drawback at times —they cannot suffer fools around them. This may make them appear uncharitable at times, but is the result of their strong desire for efficiency.

Constitutionally, Aquarians are never really the most robust of people. They are inclined to suffer from rheumatism, and their circulation frequently leaves much to be desired, but if natural preventatives and restoratives are taken in youth, these are often found to be most effective.

The following are my "luck-bringers" for the Aquarian types:

The colors thought to be best suited and lucky for them are normally either blacks or blues.

The jewel they should wear if possible should be their birthstone, which is the amethyst.

The day of the week most likely to be successful for working out any problem is a Monday or a Thursday.

The month may be any one of three—June, September or October—but never April or May.

Marriage is never hurried into by an Aquarian. They give it a lot of thought, but when they do marry, they make extremely loyal and very attentive mates. They invariably find their greatest happiness with either a Gemini (born between May 21st and June 20th) or a Libran (born between September 22nd and October 22nd).

Should their marriage partner be a Gemini, they can expect this person to be very intelligent, yet at times extremely stubborn. It will be best to bear in mind that there may be times when it will be advisable to impart an idea so skillfully that the Gemini mind may regard it as his own. Then the idea will be accepted with enthusiasm. Geminis love encourgement and praise.

If, on the other hand, an Aquarian chooses to tie up with a Libran subject, he may be in for some irritating times. Librans endeavor to be fair and just to such a degree at times that it can wear the patience of Job. They are also extremely generous, sometimes at the cost of those nearest and dearest to them. With a Libran, it is essential to admit it openly if any mistake is made or fib spoken. A Libran will nearly always forgive any fault which is admitted, but woe betide anyone who is "found out."

## PISCES—February 19th to March 20th

Pisces is the twelfth and last sign of the Zodiac; those born under this sign are invariably easy to impress because they are so extremely receptive and consequently are often successful mediums. While they are persistent, they are rarely positive in their actions, and their emotions are liable to make them too susceptible to other people's ideas and reactions.

Depression is certainly not an unknown quality to them, for when a worry, no matter how trivial, hits them they are apt to sink to a very low level. When they are without cares, they are excellent companions. Kindness is one of their strongest attributes. Show a Piscean an underdog, and sympathy, patience and generosity will absolutely shine through on the underdog's behalf. (Also, they are great lovers of animals.)

When the Piscean gets depressed, he grumbles very little; rather he remains quiet and suffers in a martyrlike fashion. Pisceans are likely to have financial peculiarities inasmuch as at times they are almost fanatical in their desire to save a few pennies while at other times they will happily spend money like water. Born under the dual sign of Pisces (the Fishes) it is quite possible for these people to show the two extremes of their character at the same time.

Pisceans are ever ready to take on heavy responsibilities provided that they are convinced that these responsibilities will serve a useful purpose. They hate failures and because they fear anything which may give them cause to fret, they nearly always put forward a strong front.

Those born in February are ambitious and like to be recognized for their good qualities. They make really wonderful hosts. Owing to their extreme caution, however, when it comes to taking chances in life, they quite often miss opportunities where their personal ambitions are concerned.

The people who are born between March 1st and 10th do have to put up with quite a number of domestic bothers usually brought about by their own temperament. This type more often than not lives in a world of his own at times, and good fortune sometimes takes its time before coming his way.

Those born between March 11th and 20th are the ones with the most confidence in themselves. They are apt to hold quite a good opinion of their capabilities, but they are not always practical in their approach to problems. However, give them something that is difficult to explain and they will analyze this much more deeply than others. These Pisceans are nice, but restless types.

You will normally find that those born under this sign make the best caterers, nurses, teachers and fashion leaders. Whatever they do, they like to feel that it will benefit others.

Constitutionally, the Piscean has average health, but by avoiding extremes and keeping to a regular pattern of life and diet, he can maintain a fairly good record of all-round health. Disorders of the blood are the one thing that may trouble him most.

From experience, I have learned that the "luck-bringers" for those born under this sign, are likely to be:

The colors of blue, purple and mauve.

The jewel they should wear most frequently should be their birthstone, the bloodstone.

The day of importance for them in any week is usually either a Tuesday or a Saturday.

The month (or months) most likely to be unusually favorable to them cannot be singled out, for in the case of Pisceans, during the coming year, for instance, good fortune appears to be distributed throughout, with slightly more favorable indications during the early months.

Marriage: Pisceans would do well to remember that they mate best with Cancer subjects (June 21st to July 21st) or with Scorpions (born between October 23rd and November 21st).

Should they choose to marry a Cancer type, then they must expect this person to be unusually ambitious in business and possessed of a really keen sense of humor. The Cancer subject cannot be pushed for he is stubborn and has a temper. Persuade him, however, in the right way, and his generosity knows no bounds.

On the other hand, if the choice of marriage partner should be a Scorpio subject, then a Piscean may be sure of devotion plus, at times, an irritating possessiveness. This type will at times attempt to keep his partner in "a glass case," thinking only of his mate's protection, and the Lord help any other person who is thought by the Scorpion to be trying to harm that mate. Try to think before making any impulsive statements to Scorpions, for they have elephantlike memories, especially when annoyed, and at all times remember that, whereas it is quite possible to persuade a Scorpion to see your point of view if possibilities are discussed quietly between you, anger and sharp retorts will get you nowhere.

# Chapter II

## ★ TELEPATHY ★

Once regarded as "far out," along with astrology, telepathy is now being established, even in laboratories, as a scientifically valid human attribute. Telepathy is thought transference other than by means of any of the five senses. If you can develop your telepathic ability, you will have gone far toward uncovering the prophetic power in yourself.

A friend asked me quite recently if I had heard from an acquaintance of many years standing, whom I had not seen over a long period of time; I said that I had not, and did not know whether he was still alive. By the very next post, I received a letter from him. My feeling was that at the time of his writing this letter, he quite obviously had me and our mutual friend very much in mind, and that in turn must have transferred to the mutual friend's mind, so that we found ourselves, quite out of the blue, thinking about him.

How often have you heard of a mother knowing that her child was in danger or sick when she was many, many miles away from that child, or a twin sensing the unhappiness of the other twin and knowing him to be unhappy, though at a distance? While I do not believe that you can transfer the actual words of a thought, I do believe that if the link between you and someone else is strong enough, then by sitting quietly and concentrating, you can send a message to someone whom you care for—many miles distant—by this simple act of telepathy.

My own mother, during the First World War, woke in the night and saw a dear friend of hers who was away fighting in Flanders; she had had a dream that he was crossing a bridge, and she could hear gunfire; in her high state of emotion, she screamed out to him to go back and walk under the bridge. When he returned some two years later, he informed us that he had been crossing a bridge, under heavy fire at that time, and that he had had the strangest compulsion to turn back and walk under the bridge. He did so, even though the firing under the bridge was equally as heavy; most of the boys who had gone over that bridge had been shot or maimed.

I know of a lady who disliked a very well-known band conductor in England; in her own words, "I used to sit and will him to fall, or have great tiredness of his legs while conducting his orchestra on important occasions." I knew this conductor quite well; he told me that one night when he had to play before the king and queen of England, he found himself at times having to hold onto the rostrum for fear that his legs would give way beneath him. Yet as soon as the concert was over, he was in perfectly fit condition once again, and when he went to consult a medical specialist about this, the latter could find absolutely nothing wrong with him physically.

I give you these very few short examples in order to demonstrate that three things must exist for telepathy to work. First, a great closeness of one kind or another with the person to whom you are sending out a telepathic message or from whom you are receiving a telepathic message. Second, a certain amount of extrasensory perception (but then, as I have said so many times before, I believe that every one of us has extrasensory perception). And third, on these occasions, the mind must be completely free of other matters, and to a certain extent, able to concentrate, consciously or unconsciously, when one is attempting to will such messages over long distances. There is very little more basically that one can tell about telepathy now. Of course, I could go into many more experiences of which I know, but that would only add to the authenticity of the cases that I have already related.

I would suggest to you that, if you wish to try and make telepathy come about, please do not try to force it, but let it come naturally, and please do not attempt this on complete strangers, for I can assure you that it will not work.

# Chapter III

# ★ THE ANALYSIS OF
#          DREAMS ✶

Dreams have long been key factors in telepathic and prophetic experiences. Their relevance to both is now under intensive study.

We can be fairly certain when we say that we each have two lives: one that is our daytime wakefulness, and the other, the life that we enter when we have retired to bed and are sleeping. While there are quite a few of us who dream fairly regularly in this sleeping state and remember our dreams, others apparently only dream occasionally— but this happens to all of God's creatures. How often have you seen your cat or your dog either moving his legs as though he were running, or whimpering and sometimes even giving an occasional cry when he is in fact fast asleep?

Sometimes we have nightmares. Some doctors maintain that they generally occur when a person is lying on his back, and rarely happen if a person is lying on his right side. I have often advised a client to try a small exercise in order to get a more satisfactory night's sleep. I tell him to lie on his back until he is slightly sleepy, then to turn to his left side until he begins to doze, and always, at this stage, to turn onto his right side, and settle down to a good night's sleep.

I advise this for two reasons. First, as I have said, so that he will eventually sleep lying on his right side, and thus get a more beneficial night's rest, but second, because trying to remember this exercise will have the effect of stopping him from thinking about what has been happening throughout his day and what he thinks is going to happen tomorrow, or what he is going to be saying (which invariably he never will anyhow). In other words, to stop worrying about things that he can do very little about. By using this exercise, he will get a good night's rest, and thus be able to think more clearly the next day.

Some of our dreams are so mixed up that they may mean very little, in any clear way; many can be caused by indigestion. Others, which we cannot recall at all the next day, I strongly feel must arise from the impressions received during the previous day, or what we think we ought to be doing in the near future. But those dreams that stand out vividly in our memories during our waking hours are the dreams of which we should take note, because these could hold either messages for us, or warnings, or, in some cases, even strong guidance for future events.

One thing we have got to have absolutely clear in our minds is the fact that we should divide our dreams into three kinds. First, dreams of what we should have done at some time or another; second, ambitious dreams for our own personal aims; and third, the extremely impressive dreams which at the time may make little sense to us, but which are, of course, of the most importance. During these dreams, it is possible for us to appear to be engaged in real life and actually doing whatever is taking place in the dream; after dreams like this, if we have enjoyed them, we can at times wake up quite suddenly and then try to sleep again with the sole purpose of attempting to recapture what we were dreaming about in order to see what the ultimate result of the dream will be. On the other hand, we can find ourselves waking up very abruptly, in a highly emotional state, because a dream has greatly terrified us—then we are a little frightened of going to sleep again, for fear that this dream may again impress its frightening aspects on us.

My strong belief—and one I have always held—is that each and every one of us is, to varying degrees, psychic; dreams can contain insights, for good or bad, which we are unable to bring to our minds during our waking hours, and many dreams *are* future happenings that are casting their shadows.

The very famous American clairvoyant Edgar Cayce was known as the "Sleeping Prophet" because he used to put himself into a self-induced sleep—and while sleeping, he would talk to his wife or secretary about a person unknown to his waking self. His listeners would record what Cayce said, and in many, many cases, his diagnoses and prognostications in this sleeping state were absolutely correct.

Dreams can give us warnings, they can give us advice on how to cope with things or people, and they can give us great encouragement. I shall now list for you some of the major images about which one can dream. If you use your imagination subtly, you should be able to come to your own conclusions as to the meanings as I have experienced them.

## Age

If you see yourself as older than you actually are and also others around you as older, this denotes that you may be about to become ill—but because you have seen other people who are aged around you, you will know that you will recover. If you see yourself in a dream as you were when much younger, then you would do well to try not to irritate people who are around you; otherwise, you could be due for a slight conflict.

## An Accident

To dream of an accident is in itself a warning that you need to take a little more care where your business affairs are concerned. If the accident takes place away from where you live and not in a town well known to you, it could indicate a slight setback where a love affair is concerned.

## An Anchor

An anchor is usually a steadying symbol in a dream. If

the anchor is on clear land, you can be fairly certain you
will soon have peace of mind, security and good luck. But
if the anchor is in water and submerged, while this is not
bad, it does forewarn you of a few disappointments
through delays or frustrations.

## Anger

Now this is a dream that you can very nearly always
reverse in interpretation, for if you dream that you are
really angry with someone who is close to you or whom
you love, it indicates how good that person is for you, and
how loyal he will be to you. On the other hand, if you
do not know the person with whom you are angry in your
dream, but can see him, you can expect some very pleasing news to reach you within a short period.

## Animals

All animals seen in dreams are not good; some may represent enemies or bad friends—with the exception of a
horse, which means that you have a very good and de-
voted person around you. If the horse, however, appears
to be slightly excited, you could have a few business difficulties to get through before you reach success.

## Apples

To see apples in a dream is always an extremely good
sign, provided that you do not see yourself eating them;
just to see apples indicates some very good fortune for
you, whereas to be eating one could foretell a disappointment in the near future.

## A Balcony

To dream of yourself standing on a balcony, or of other
people standing on a balcony, while not terribly serious,
does in effect tell you that you have got to face up to a
few difficulties that are standing in your way for the moment.

### A Bath

If you dream that of yourself either in a bath or standing beside a bath that holds clean water, you will know that anything of importance in which you are engaged at that moment should meet with success. Should the water be used or not clean, you had better muster yourself in preparation for a few troubles which might come your way.

### A Bed

If you see yourself making up a bed in your dream, and when you have made it up, you sit on it, this should mean that there is marriage in the air for you, and in consequence, you will move to a new place. On the other hand, if you dream that you are in a hotel bed or a bed that is strange to you, this indicates that difficulties you have been going through will now take a very definite turn for the better.

### Bills

If, in your dream, you see yourself going around paying bills, you can reverse your feeling about this and expect some financial gains for yourself. On the other hand, should you find yourself being worried in your dreams because you have some bills which you have not paid, this means that there may be someone around you who is not talking too nicely about you.

### A Birth

To dream of a birth, if you are not married, does indicate a little trouble in the very near future for you. If, however, you are married, then it is an excellent sign for future security.

### Blood

Blood is not a good thing to dream about in any way,

for it has three potential meanings: first, quarrels; second, disappointments; and third, affairs of the heart going slightly wrong for you.

## Books

If you dream that you are either buying a book or looking at a row of books, this is excellent, for it means a great deal of future happiness through learning for you; the more books you see, the better the portents indicated are.

## A Bottle

If you see yourself in your dream drinking from a full bottle, this is an extremely good sign, denoting success and luck; if, on the other hand, you knock the bottle over and lose some of the liquid in it, you can expect to have a few angry words in your home.

## Bread

This is a sign of great contentment; if you see yourself eating bread in your dream, this denotes that you are going to be in extremely good health.

## Breaking Something

To dream that you are breaking something or that someone around you has dropped and broken something you like very much is not the best of omens, for this means that either the health of someone close to you or your own health is not going to be quite up to scratch.

## A Bride

To dream that you see yourself or someone close to you as a bride is not good; this can either mean a big disappointment or a letdown for you.

### A Brush

Should you see yourself painting or brushing anything in a dream, you will know that something that you have wanted for quite a long period will definitely, and very happily for you, come your way.

### A Building

Judge a dream of this image according to the size of the building that you see in your dream. If it is a building of ordinary size, this indicates a change or changes about to come your way; but if the building is very large, you will be meeting a great success in the future.

### A Burglar

This is not good because it means that you may expect deceit and disloyalty from someone whom you trust a great deal.

### A Cake

To dream that you see a festive cake, such as a birthday, wedding or anniversary cake, is extremely good, for not only does it denote that your circumstances are going to be happy, but also that you are going to enjoy good health.

### Calling a Name

Should you hear someone calling you, this is indeed a happy omen, especially in the romantic field. On the other hand, should you hear yourself calling someone else's name, this is a person usually who stands in very good stead toward you.

### A Candle

This image has two likely meanings. First, if you find that you are unable to light a candle in a dream, you should be on your guard against troubles around you. On the other hand, if you can light a candle, and it burns very clearly, you may take this to be a sign that you are going to be prosperous.

## A Car

This is not the best of dream symbols. If you are standing beside a car or sitting in it, but not driving it, that is a warning that you have to take care, because there could be slight trouble in store for you. If, on the other hand, you are driving a car, this indicates that you may undergo a loss.

## A Carpet

To dream that you are walking on a very good carpet is extremely fortunate; the more luxurious the carpet, the greater your good fortune.

## A Cascade of Water

To dream that you are standing by a cascade of water is not good, for it indicates that you could be disappointed with your efforts. Should you see someone you know either being drenched by this cascade or even walking into it, you will know that that person is being unwise in his behavior and is courting trouble.

## A Cat

I personally love cats, but they are considered to be sly, and if you see one in your dream, this is nearly always an indication that you are trusting someone who is extremely deceitful to you, so take care.

## A Cathedral

If you are standing outside a cathedral, or even a church, talking or admiring the building, it is considered to be very lucky, but if you walk into that cathedral, this indicates that your peace of mind is going to be slightly troubled, and is a warning to you to sit on the fence in most respects for a short while.

## A Cemetery

Surprisingly, if you just see yourself, in a cemetery, this is very good, because it denotes that you are going to make excellent headway in most things going on around you. On the other hand, if while in a cemetery, you see a loved one who was close to you but whom you have lost, then the old saying applies—to dream of the dead means trouble with the living.

## A Chain, Gold or Silver

When you see a woman who is wearing a gold or silver chain around her neck, this denotes that you could be about to receive a gift from someone who cherishes you greatly. On the other hand, should a gold or silver chain turn out, on closer inspection, to be a heavy, binding type of chain, then you will know that something that is worrying you will turn out all right.

## Choking

To dream that you are choking and cannot catch your breath means just the opposite from what you might think: it is indeed an extremely lucky dream for you personally.

## Cigarettes

To dream that someone gives you a light for a cigarette denotes that you are going to receive help from someone in a new venture. If, throughout your dream, you are smoking furiously, and then find that you have reached the butt-end of your cigarette, this indicates that you are going to achieve an ambition of yours.

## A Cleric

If you dream that you are talking with a parson, this is

not good; it's a warning of disappointments and frustrations in store for you.

## A Clock Chiming

To dream that you hear a clock chime or strike is extremely good; the louder the chime, the more comfortable are the indications for your future life.

## Colors

To dream that you see a myriad of colors is usually an indication of prosperity and success. The only two colors that are not considered to be fortunate are black and red.

## Cooking

To dream that you are cooking a meal is an indication that you should watch your health, especially in the chest and digestive area.

## Corn or Barley

To dream of corn or barley indicates that you will never want for either bread or money; the more plentiful the corn, the greater are your financial prospects.

## A Cottage

If you see yourself walking up a path in order to enter a cottage, this is a good and lucky dream; but if you see yourself coming out of a cottage in a hurry, while not particularly unlucky, certainly denotes that you have a few worries ahead of you.

## A Crab

When you see a crab in a dream, this is a warning that you have to take great care, for you could be found out in something that you are doing which is not quite legal.

## A Cross

To dream that you see or handle a cross means that there could be conflict or unhappiness in your emotional life.

## A Cup

The fuller the cup which you handle in a dream, the greater is likely to be your success. On the other hand, if a cup in a dream is absolutely empty, this is a sign of shortage.

## A Curtain

If there is a curtain in front of you in a dream, and you pull it to one side in order to go through into a room or in order to let light into a room, this means that you are going to find out that you are trusting deceitful people too much—but because you have moved the curtain to one side, you will have found out in good time.

## A Cycle

If you see a bicycle or motorcycle in your dream, or if you are riding one, this indicates that although you will eventually be quite successful you should not be pushing things in too much of a hurry for the time being.

## Dancing

To dream of yourself dancing is an excellent financial sign. It also indicates that plans about which you are ambitious should turn out really well. If you are dancing with someone and enjoying yourself, then this could denote luck for the person with whom you are dancing.

## Danger

To dream of danger is not a bad dream, for the greater your danger, the more success you can expect. If you find you have just missed danger in a dream, then you should take this as a slight warning.

### A Dentist or Teeth

This denotes that you should take care of your health because you could find yourself becoming slightly under the weather.

### The Devil

To dream of the devil, while not really bad, means that you are going to have frustrations that could last quite a while.

### A Diamond

To dream that you are handling a diamond or diamonds is not good; it's a forewarning of a slight domestic upheaval coming your way.

### A Diary

To dream that you are keeping a diary is not a good thing, for it denotes that you are either jealous or too possessive of someone around you, or vice versa.

### Diving (Swimming)

To dream that you have been swimming and that you come out in order to take a dive into the water is a warning to you not to gamble and to avoid business risks; otherwise, you could be on the losing end of a deal.

### A Doctor

To dream that you are visiting a doctor means just the reverse of what you might think: it denotes that your health is going to be good, and that you should be meeting with success in other fields as well.

### A Duck

To dream of a duck is an extremely fortunate omen, but if the duck pecks you in the dream, this indicates slight deceit where your working life is concerned.

### To Dust

If you dream that you are dusting a certain piece of furniture, this indicates that while you are undergoing quite a struggle with things around you, the more you persevere, the more chance you will have of things eventually working out well for you.

### Earth

If you dream of earth, and it appears to be good soil, this indicates an abundance of good things in store for you, but if the earth of which you dream is all parched and dried up, this indicates that you are being dishonest with yourself and at the same time, extravagant; it should warn you to mend your ways in this direction.

### An Egg

To dream of an egg or eggs, as long as they are perfect, is a good sign, for it means you will increase your worldly belongings. Should an egg be cracked or broken, this could indicate either an upcoming loss or a burglary.

### An Elopement

To dream that you are eloping or that someone you know is eloping means that a person of whom you are extremely fond could be having an association with someone who wishes you harm. Should you dream of a relative or close friend eloping, if he or she is already married, it could indicate the birth of a child in his family.

## Entertaining

This is a lucky kind of dream, providing that you are enjoying yourself in the dream. Should you not be enjoying yourself, then it is a warning for you to take care, for things may be about not to go too well for you. Should you find yourself being taken away from a party before you really wish to go in a dream, this indicates that you could lose a good opportunity through someone else's poor behavior.

## Evil

To dream of evil is not to have a bad dream, but it does mean that you should keep your eyes open where your working life is concerned, for there could be someone who does not wish you well.

## An Explosion

If you dream that you witness an explosion or are involved in an explosion, although not bad for you, does indicate that you could hear some rather unhappy news about someone of whom you think a great deal.

## Eye Glasses (Spectacles)

This dream symbol indicates that you are going to be seeing things in a much clearer light, and that, because of this, your business interests will increase in a very good way.

## Eyes

To dream that you are looking at someone, if his or her eyes stand out more than his face itself, is indicative of great good luck for you. It also denotes that a change you have in mind should come about in the near future. If you, in your dream, find that your own eyes are aching or that you have got something in an eye and find difficulty in getting it out, this is a warning of someone not being entirely truthful to you.

## A Face

If you find yourself surrounded by a lot of new faces that you do not know, this indicates either a change in where you live or a trip you are likely to take. If you dream of a happy, laughing face, this denotes that you have an extremely good friend around you who will be willing to support you.

## A Fair

If you dream that you are attending a fair, and even participating in some of the fun of the fair, this is not a very lucky dream for you personally.

## Fame

If you dream that you are famous, or that someone you know has become famous, unfortunately you'll have to reverse the apparent portent of this dream, because it is a warning of bad luck.

## Fat (Obesity)

This is not a lucky thing to dream about, especially for a female.

## A Father

If you see your father in a dream, whether he is alive or dead, this is an indication of some great happiness coming your way. If he does not attempt to speak to you, then that is a slight warning that you can expect a little bother.

## Fear

To dream that you are frightened is, when interpreted, a portent of just the opposite, for it means that you are going to be happy and courageous.

## A Fiancé

If you dream about your fiancé in any way, this usually indicates that there could be a slight disagreement between you, but that you will patch it up.

## Fighting

If you dream that you are in the middle of a fight with someone else, but that you are getting the better of this person, this indicates that you have some difficulties to overcome, but should succeed after a struggle.

## Filming

If you see yourself being filmed, or filming either a scene or other people, this is indicative of travel which may i , over quite a distance, but about which you should keep quiet and not chatter.

## A Fire

To dream of a fire indicates quarrels and irritations, but if you, in such a dream, are able to douse the fire, then you can expect to have good news which you had not thought you would receive.

## A Fireside

When you see yourself alone, or with people you like sitting around a fireside, this is an extremely good indication and means that prosperity is ahead of you.

## Fish

If you see a fish swimming in clear water, then you can expect good fortune in anything that you are doing. If, however, either you or someone you know catches a fish, then this tells you that you have a false friend around you somewhere.

### A Fleet

Not always good, but if you see ships making for port, you will prevail over other people who may be difficult with you.

### Flirting

If you are flirting in a dream, you can take this to be quite a happy and lucky sign, but if you are flirting with evil intent, then you could be shedding a few tears.

### Flowers

Flowers mean serenity and happiness; if you find yourself picking them in a dream, this indicates that your friends are very loyal toward you. If you are throwing away flowers, that means that you will be having a quarrel with someone in the very near future, and in effect, the dream is a slight warning to you to try to avoid this.

### Flying

Although it is not bad to dream you are flying high into the air at a great speed, it does strongly indicate that you are possibly living beyond your means and should economize a little.

### Food

If you dream you are eating a meal and thoroughly enjoying it, this is lucky, for it means that you are going to derive satisfaction from the plans you have laid.

### A Forest

The prophetic meaning of this dream symbol relates to the density of the forest; if it is very thick so that you find yourself having to grope your way through it, this could mean bad luck and that some of your faults may be brought home very forcibly to you. On the other hand, if you come out of a forest into a clearing, that tells you that even though you are going through a slightly difficult time, things will improve.

## Fretting

To dream that you are fretting or worrying means just the opposite, for it foretells good news and great peace of mind for you.

## Fruit

To dream of fruit is generally good; if a woman is pregnant and she sees among the fruit an apple, it is likely that she will give birth to a male child. Berries, on the other hand, indicate both disappointment and annoyances.

## Frying

If you are preparing a meal and cooking it in a frying pan, this could indicate a completely unnecessary and silly quarrel with someone in the near future.

## Fur

To dream of fur is considered to be extremely fortunate. If, on the other hand, the fur is slightly wet, that indicates that you will gain good fortune by making a change of some description around you.

## Gain

If you see yourself making a lot of gains in a dream, through income or otherwise, take care, for this can indicate that someone is going to deceive and cheat you.

## Galloping

If you are riding a horse at a steady gallop and there are no obstacles in your way, then you can expect to meet up with some pleasing success in the very near future.

## Gambling

When you dream you are gambling, it is a warning to you to act on your own initiative and not be dogmatically led by others around you.

## A Garden

To dream that you find yourself in a beautiful garden is one of the luckiest dreams you can have, as far as money is concerned.

## Gasoline

This is not a good thing to dream about, for it usually indicates quarrels and arguments, and bad feeling with those around you.

## Gems

To see a number of gems, or to be wearing them, while not really bad, is not a fortunate indication for you.

## A Giant

Should you dream you meet a giant, this tells you that you have got to muster up all your courage and determination, for by so doing, you will overcome the obstacles that are around you.

## A Gift

If someone you know presents you with a gift in a dream, then you would be well advised not to trust that person completely, for it could mean that they are slightly shifty by nature.

## Gloominess

When gloominess abounds in a dream, it is an indication than an opportunity for betterment is going to come your way and that you should grasp it without hesitation.

## God

If you dream that you are in communication with God, this indicates peace of mind, happiness and great stability for you.

## Grief

To dream of grief denotes great joy and a lot of laughter coming your way.

## A Gun

If you hear and see a gun being fired in a dream, it means that you may be told that someone of whom you think a lot is ill, but if you are firing the gun yourself, this is a warning for you to take more care or you could be the one who may become sick.

## Hair

As long as the hair you see looks healthy and well groomed, this is a very successful dream for future prospects, but if you are worried about the condition of your hair in a dream, this indicates that you'll have to concentrate harder in order to get over difficulties going on around you.

## A Hall

If you dream that you are in a house that has a very big hall, and it is not your own house, this denotes that you are going to have to make up your mind rather quickly about something which could alter other things around you.

## A Ham

While this is not particularly significant, it is invariably quite a lucky dream symbol.

## A Handkerchief

If you are searching for a handkerchief, and cannot find it, this could mean that someone close to you is going away for a period, but if you find the handkerchief easily, then you can expect a pleasing present.

## Happiness

To dream that you are extremely happy is not good. It warns you to take care for the time being. If you dream that someone close to you is hilariously happy, then you would do well to tell him to look for difficulties where his work is concerned.

## Headaches

If you are suffering from a headache in a dream, this means that you are going to have to persevere more than you have been with a person or things around you, because he or they can present difficulties.

## Heart

This image is extremely good; if you see another person as well, it is an indication that that person holds a great deal of genuine affection for you.

## Heels

If you see the heel of your shoe breaking or if the heel of your shoe is causing you pain, then you'll have a few worries to contend with in the near future.

## Herbs

If you dream that you can either see herbs growing or are mixing herbs while cooking, this can be taken as an extremely good sign; you should be receiving some very encouraging news in the near future.

## To Hide

When you dream that you are hiding from someone or something, this foreshadows that some rather annoying news is on its way to you.

## A Hill

If you dream you are trying to climb a hill, but are not making very good progress, this indicates that you have a few obstacles ahead, and that now is not the time to try to get over them. On the other hand, if you find yourself climbing a hill with great ease, then you may know that you are going to surmount your obstacles and that both changes and good fortune lie ahead of you.

## A Hog

When you dream of either a hog or two or three hogs in a sty, this means success and luck for your future; but if the hog either looks ill or attempts to attack you, then look out for either a lean time or some bad luck.

## An Honor

If you dream of an honor being bestowed on someone near or dear to you, this is a warning that he or she has got to be rather careful; economy should be a keynote for him. The same would apply to yourself if you dreamed that you received an honor.

## A Horseshoe

If you see a horseshoe, with the open end up, this indicates a lengthy journey across water. If, however, you *find* a horseshoe, or have one given to you, then this means that you could receive an inheritance.

## Icicles

This is always indicative of great happiness, especially in the romantic area.

### Income

If you dream that you are going to have a raise in your income, it is not a good sign; it warns you to be careful.

### An Infant

To dream that you have an infant or are tending an infant, who is happy, is an extremely good dream. If, however, the child is unwell, then this is a slight warning that there could be a few bothers in store for you.

### An Injury

To dream that you have met with an injury warns you to take care, but if you dream that someone you know has injured you, then you would do well to keep your own confidence where this person is concerned, because at the moment you cannot trust him.

### An Inn (Hotel)

This can denote a journey for you, but if you are having difficulty in your dream (in getting booked into an inn, for example), then this denotes that you should think twice about making changes for the moment.

### Insanity

This may not necessarily be a vivid dream image. It could, of course, be from tiredness. However, when it clearly is a strong dream symbol, it is an excellent sign, for it indicates great success ahead of you.

### Insects

To dream that you can see insects around you, while not bad, does mean that you can expect a few delays or disappointments in your general affairs.

### An Insult

This has two meanings. First, difficulties could be coming your way which may take a little surmounting. Secondly, it can indicate that a change is coming your way either in your home or where your work is concerned.

## An Invalid

Provided that you are the invalid in your dream, but are getting better, you will know that you are surmounting recent difficulties and are on the way to greater peace of mind. If, however, you appear to be having a struggle to get well, then this indicates still a few more obstacles to be overcome.

## Ironing

To dream that you are ironing and smoothing things out means almost what you see—that you are entering better times and can expect greater cooperation from those around you.

## Itching

To dream that you are itching and scratching yourself is an extremely good dream, for it means you are worrying about things quite unnecessarily.

## A Jacket

To dream that you are wearing a new jacket, or going to buy one, means that your patience is about to be rewarded, because a good opportunity is coming your way.

## A Jail

This dream image can be taken to be a slight warning of ill-health.

## Jars

The fuller the jar of which you dream, the greater will be your good fortune; this is always thought to be a lucky dream, even if the jar or jars are empty.

### Jeopardy

For you to dream that you are in slight jeopardy indicates that both good opportunities and great good fortune are coming your way.

### Jewels

With the exception of emeralds, all jewels, whether you are giving or receiving them, are considered to be very lucky to dream about. Emeralds give you warning that you will need to take care with someone very close to you.

### Jilted

If you find yourself worried and upset in a dream because you have been jilted, this indicates just how very genuine the person of your choice will prove himself to be.

### A Jockey

For a woman to dream of a jockey racing means that she is going to have an offer of an engagement or marriage, but for a man to dream about this is not so fortunate.

### A Journey

Whether it be a long or short journey you find yourself taking in a dream, it means that you can expect changes in your present way of living.

### Jumping

Not the best of dream images, for here jumps may be considered to symbolize difficulties that you will meet. If you jump clear, then all will be well for you.

## A Jungle

If the jungle is very dense, then you are either going to have some worry where your job is concerned or are going to be slightly in the red moneywise.

## A Kennel

To dream of a kennel means, strangely, that your nerves are not good, and that you are going to feel rather like a prisoner and could be snappy in consequence; this is a warning to try to avoid having quarrels with people around you.

## A Kettle

As long as the water in the kettle is not boiling over, this is considered to be a lucky dream. If the water is boiling furiously, then you could be losing a treasured possession.

## A Key

To dream that you add a new key to your key chain indicates a change of residence for you, but to dream that you lose a key is not a fortunate omen.

## A Kick

Though it seems otherwise, this is a good indication should you dream that you are kicking someone, but if you are on the receiving end of a kick, then you have a rather vicious enemy.

## A King

Royal dreams are always lucky; if you dream either that you are being sociable with a king or that a king smiles at you, you are in for a period of extremely good luck.

### A Kiss

To dream that you are kissing someone whom you do not know is not a good indication. It tells you that you need to take greater care with things around you.

### A Kitten

To dream of a kitten or any baby animal is always considered to be extremely favorable.

### A Knee

To dream that you see a perfect knee, or that someone admires your knee, is considered to be fortunate, but if you dream that you have hurt your kneecap, this means that you will need a lot of perseverance, because a few worries and troubles are coming your way.

### A Knife

To dream about a knife is not a good omen, for it means misunderstandings with people you like, and can sometimes indicate tears.

### Knitting

To dream that you are knitting a jumper or cardigan, etc., is extremely good, for it is very indicative of good fortune. However, should you find that you keep dropping your stitches, this means that you have someone around you who is not genuine and could cause you depression.

### A Label

To dream that you are writing out a label, or sticking or typing a label onto a box or case, denotes that a pleasant surprise is coming your way.

## A Ladder

To dream that you are happily climbing up a ladder is extremely good, for it indicates that you are going to be making greater headway toward your ambitions, but if you find that you are frightened to climb the ladder because of height or if you see a ladder falling, this is not a fortunate sign.

## A Lake

To dream that you see a beautiful clear lake indicates that your patience is about to pay off, and your life is now going to take on a very pleasant hue. If, however, the lake is not clear and the surroundings are gloomy, this denotes that you still have a few difficulties to go through.

## Lateness

To dream that no matter how much you are trying to be somewhere in time, you find yourself very late, denotes that you are well thought of, especially where your ideas are concerned, and that others around you will be seeking your advice.

## Laundry

To dream that you are laundering something is not a good omen; it means that you will meet up with a few reversals.

## The Law

It is not considered lucky to dream about the law or a lawyer, or to dream that you are taking legal action, because it forewarns you to think twice where your commitments and finances are concerned.

## Lessons

If you dream that you are being given lessons in any

particular field and are enjoying them, you can expect a great deal of success in the fields that interest you.

## A Letter

To dream that you either receive or write a letter is to know that you can expect news that will come as a surprise to you in the near future.

## A Lie

To dream that you are being told lies by someone near to you is quite good, for the person whom you see telling you the lie is genuine about you. However, if you yourself have to tell a lie, this is not good, for it means that you could find yourself bothered by others around you.

## A Line

To dream that you are in a line means that you are going to renew an acquaintance or make up a quarrel, and that great happiness with the other person will follow.

## Littleness

To dream that either you or someone close to you is little in stature is good, for it indicates that you will be making good headway in most of what you do as your life goes on.

## Loans

To dream that you are being asked to lend something foretells of losses to come your way.

## Locks

To dream that you are either locking things up or that you cannot get into a door or cupboard because it is locked and there is no sign of the key is not the best of dreams; it means that not only have you got to economize a little more than you have been doing, but that a secret is being kept from you.

### Magic

When you dream that magical things are happening either to you or around you, this is indicative of beneficial changes coming your way, when you had thought that they could not possibly do so.

### A Man

It is always very lucky to dream of a man, especially if he is a stranger to you, but it is not quite so lucky to dream of meeting a new lady.

### A Mansion

To dream that you see yourself in a grand mansion is not good, for it means that you have a slightly troublesome period to go through.

### A Map

To dream that you are reading a map usually denotes that you have changes in mind, either for work or for where you live, and that you will be making them.

### A Mask

To dream that you are wearing a mask means that you are being slightly deceitful to someone around you and that this could cause you unhappiness eventually. On the other hand, should someone else around you be wearing a mask in a dream, then that person is being slightly treacherous toward you.

### A Master

To dream of the person you work for or to dream that you yourself become the master is always good, and means that you could be prospering.

## Meat

It is not good to dream that you are eating meat, or even to dream that you are attending a festive board, although it may be considered quite lucky if you yourself are preparing the meal.

## Medicine

While not the luckiest of dream symbols, this does denote, especially if you are taking the medicine yourself, that you are getting through most of your problems successfully.

## Merriment

If you are enjoying yourself enormously in a dream, then you can, funnily enough, expect a few difficulties to come your way in the near future.

## Mice

This is not a good dream image, because it indicates that you are trusting someone, of whom you see quite a lot, far too much.

## Money

Whether you dream you are paying money out or receiving it, this is an extremely good sign. If you *find* some money, an opportunity that you have been hoping for may be slightly delayed. If you win money or find yourself having to borrow it, this is not good and means you should take great care for a while.

## A Muddle

Should you dream you find yourself in a muddle, this is not bad; it is merely a warning that you should watch out for slight accidents which could come your way.

## Music

To hear music, especially if it is melodic, is always considered to be extremely lucky; it indicates success in most of what is going on around you.

## Mustard

To dream that you are putting mustard on food or even tasting it is not good, for it means that you must keep your own counsel and try to avoid chatter.

## To Nag

If you are either being nagged or are doing the nagging in a dream, this indicates chatter ahead which can be either pleasing or annoying, but mainly it forewarns you that you must for the time being keep your own confidences.

## Nakedness

To dream that you are either walking about naked or even swimming naked is considered to be extremely lucky for you, especially if you are unmarried and in love, for it indicates great loyalty from your opposite number and a good deal of happiness.

## Names

If you hear your own name being called by someone in a dream, this indicates that your help is going to be asked for in the near future, but if you hear someone talking about someone close to you and mentioning his name, then this means that you could have a little unhappiness from an emotional source.

## Neck

If someone admires your neck in a dream, this indicates that a current love affair is going to be extremely good, but if you are wearing something around your neck and it breaks, this means that you can expect affairs not to go well for the time being in your domestic life.

## Negatives

If you are studying negatives or photographs in a dream, this means that you will be needing all your concentration in order to be one step ahead of others, so that you do not meet with failure.

## News

This is a dream image that you'll have to reverse in interpreting prophetically, for if the news you hear in a dream is good, then you could have a slight worry ahead of you, but if it is bad, then it means good luck, but nothing outstanding.

## Night

To dream that it is nighttime and that you are having to grope your way around in the dark, while not being a bad dream, does forewarn you that you are going through a rather difficult period; as long as you do not get too agitated in your dream because of the circumstances, you will eventually be happy because you will come out into the light.

## Noise

If you dream that you can hardly hear what is going on around you because there is so much noise, this indicates that you are going to have to be the peacemaker with people close to you, who are not going to be seeing eye to eye.

## A Nosebleed

This is a health dream, and it means that you must take more care of yourself than you have been doing of late, and rest more.

## A Note

To dream that you are writing a very quick note and trying to get it to someone around you indicates that you are going to have to ask help from someone but cannot rely too much on obtaining it.

## A Nurse

To dream of a nurse is usually an excellent sign, because it means that you are going to be quite prosperous where your work and financial affairs are concerned.

## An Oath

To dream that you are swearing an oath, or even guaranteeing something, is always indicative of a good financial outlook for you.

## Oats

It is extremely lucky to dream of either oats or corn or anything similar, for it denotes that as long as you carry on with your general behavior, you will meet with success and happiness.

## An Obituary

To dream of death invariably means that you'll have news of someone who is living; this will be, in nine cases out of ten, good news, and can even mean that you will be giving a gift to a newly married couple.

## An Offer

If someone makes you an offer in a dream, whether it be good or not very good, it is usually a lucky indication —for it does mean that you will meet with improvements, especially in your working life.

## Oil

Generally speaking, to dream of oil is not the most fortunate dream to have, for it means that irritations, frustrations and delays could be coming your way.

## Old Age

To dream of your old age has two meanings. First, that you need more confidence in your abilities, and, second, that you have no need to worry, for you should do far better than you think in most of the things to which you set your hand.

## An Opera

To dream that you are at an opera, or that you are just listening to the music from an opera, indicates struggles lying ahead for you.

## An Optician

To dream that you are visiting an optician is indicative that you have got to keep your eyes open for opportunities, for you could so easily miss them.

## An Orange

How ripe and how sweet the orange that you are eating is makes a difference: if it is sweet and nicely ripe, then good fortune is coming your way, but if it is tough and a little sharp, you have got to take care that your words are not misconstrued by others.

## An Orphan

If you dream of orphans or even that you yourself are an orphan, you can be pretty certain that someone you have not yet met is going to prove to be an extremely good and helpful friend to you in the future.

### An Ox

When you see an ox in a dream, this is extremely lucky, but if you see more than one ox, this indicates that now is the time when you should be taking more chances in order to further your comforts.

### Pain

Pain is always considered to be a very lucky dream symbol; the more painful your dream appears, the more necessary you are going to be to others, especially those who love you, and the more happiness and success are likely to come your way.

### A Palace

To dream that you find yourself in a palace is considered to be one of the luckiest dreams emotionally, for it denotes a serene and very happy love affair.

### Paper

This is not a good dream image, for it denotes unsettledness; the cleaner the paper you see or are using in your dream, the more chance you have of getting over difficulties, but if the paper is torn or dirty, then luck is not with you for the time being and you would do well to stay calm and do nothing out of the ordinary.

### A Parcel

A small parcel that you receive or are carrying can denote that a disappointment is coming your way, but if you receive a big parcel, this is considered to be very lucky, though also indicative of changes likely to take place around you.

### A Party

If you dream that you are having an extremely good

time at a party, then you can expect some good fortune to come your way, but if the party is formal and snobbish, then you could be meeting up with slight unhappiness through your own misguided actions.

## A Peasant

To dream that you are talking to a peasant is extremely good, especially where your finances or work are concerned.

## A Pen

To dream that you are using a pen, or that you can see someone else writing a letter, means that you should be hearing news from someone you have not heard from for some time.

## Pepper

If you dream that you are using pepper or that you have got pepper in your nostrils and it is irritating them, this usually indicates that you are going to be proud and pleased by the results of the endeavors of someone close to you.

## Perfume

To dream of perfume, even if you are not using it yourself, is excellent, and if you are beginning a love affair this is always a fortunate indication that the affair will go very well.

## A Pillow

To dream of a pillow usually indicates that your own behavior can bring you slight trouble and that you'll have to take care.

## Pills

To dream that you are taking pills or that you have a

bottle of pills with you indicates travel and great enjoyment.

## A Pistol

If you see yourself firing a pistol in your dream, this is a warning that you could be looking for a change, because you will make very little headway, even after hard work, in what you are now doing.

## Police

To dream that you are dealing with the police or even talking to a policeman indicates that you can expect help with a problem that you have on hand, and that because of this help you will be able to overcome the problem.

## A Prize

To dream that you have either won a prize or are giving a prize means that you could be on the losing end of a deal because of someone's deception.

## A Quarrel

To dream that you are involved in a quarrel, while indicating that someone could be jealous of you, does denote that you are going to meet with success and good luck where your work or finances are concerned.

## A Queen

To dream of any royalty is always considered to be extremely lucky and is indicative of great help from those around you.

## A Quest

To dream that you are out on a quest denotes that you should be taking things more slowly, for you cannot help matters by taking action too quickly.

## Questions

To dream that you are asking someone questions or are being asked questions by someone usually means that you have to overcome a few difficulties, but that, if you are patient, you should be able to accomplish this.

## A Quilt

To dream of a quilt is considered to be lucky; the more luxurious or colorful the quilt, the greater should be your good fortune.

## A Race

To dream that you are witnessing a race, or even taking part in a race, is again a warning that you are trying to get out of a few difficulties which surround you at the time.

## Rain

To dream of walking through rain is not good. If this rain is just a slight drizzle, then it means you are going to have to have great patience, because there are a few frustrations around you, but if you are in a very heavy downfall of rain, then you must prepare for something that will depress you.

## A Rainbow

This nearly always indicates that a change, and an extremely lucky change at that, will take place for you in the near future.

## A Rat

A rat is not a good thing to see in a dream; it forewarns of deception and dishonesty from someone around you, unless you are being protected *from* a rat and recognize the person who is protecting you, in which case you can know that that person is very sincere toward you.

### A Razorblade

While, like scissors or a knife, this is not a bad dream image, it is an indication that you must prepare yourself for a quarrel with someone around you, and, in consequence, have patience with that person.

### A Reconciliation

If you dream that you are being reconciled with someone you have not seen eye to eye with over a long period, this means almost what it appears to, and is thus quite fortunate.

### A Rehearsal

If you dream that you are attending a rehearsal, or preparing yourself for something, this tells you that you have got a few difficulties to overcome, but that you should, after a while, come out on top.

### Religion

If you are happy in a dream about religion, this is a very good sign, albeit not too important, for it indicates tranquility. If, on the other hand, you are worried in any way religiously in a dream, that is not so fortunate.

### A Rescue

Invariably one dreams that he is being rescued when he is in a worried state of mind. All that this really means is that you should avoid anything of great importance for a short while.

### Revenge

Revenge can indicate a quarrel in which you are as much to blame as your opponent.

### Ribbons

This is a happy dream symbol and yet at the same time it tells you that you will be spending more money than you can really afford.

### A Riot

To dream that you are involved in a riot and are frightened could mean a shortage of money around you which will worry you, and in effect is advice for you to be more economical.

### A River

To see a river on a clear day with ⟨...⟩ is quite good and can indicate a journey, but if the weather is not good and the river looks slightly turbulent then you can look out for slight upsets in your ambitions.

### A Roof

Buildings generally are good things about which to dream; the higher you go up on a building, such as on a roof, the quicker will be the good fortune that is coming your way.

### Roses

It is very lucky to dream of roses, especially if they are in full bloom and beautiful, for this indicates luck in most directions, but mainly where your love life is concerned.

### Sadness

To dream of sadness is an indication that worries are about to leave you and that peaceful happiness is coming your way.

### Salt

Salt is a lucky dream symbol, especially where your finances are concerned, for it has always been said that to keep plenty of salt in your house means good money and health.

### Scissors

Rather like a dream of a sharp-edged knife, a dream of scissors is a forewarning that you have someone who is not loyal around you, and would be well advised not to let him know too much.

### A Separation

To dream that you are upset because you are separated from someone you love indicates that an ambitious plan you have in mind may not come to fruition.

### Shade

To dream that you are in the shade, that shadows are being cast around you, has two meanings. First, it can indicate that, after a struggle, your money affairs are going to improve. On the other hand, it can indicate that you are going to gain some money through a legal action or through news from a lawyer.

### Sheep

To dream that you see sheep is really very good, because it denotes that you should carry on with your ideas; they stand an excellent chance of meeting with great success.

### A Ship

To dream that you are on board a ship and can either see the harbor or are making for the harbor is considered to be lucky for most of the things that are going on around you.

## A Shop

To dream that you are either working in or the owner of a shop indicates that your affairs are temporarily slightly muddled, but if you are busy in this dream shop, this denotes that you will come out on top in the end.

## A Sigh

To dream that you are sighing is good, for it means you are due for a great deal of merriment.

## Silk

It is not often good to dream of silk for a woman, for it means she has someone who is not completely honest around her, but, for a man, silk is an extremely lucky indication regarding his business.

## Singing

To dream of singing forewarns of difficulties ahead. If you hear someone else singing in a clear voice, you will know that you have obstacles around you but that you should get over them by perseverance.

## Singleness

For a married person to dream that he is single indicates that he will be hearing some annoying chatter against himself.

## Skating

To dream that you are skating and gliding smoothly along is not a good dream and can forecast slight accidents, so take care.

## Sleep

To dream that you see yourself sleeping is not a fortunate dream.

## Smoking

To dream that you are smoking or see smoke indicates a few disappointments and frustrations for you, but see *Cigarettes* for variations.

## Snow

To dream that you see a lot of snow or have to dig snow away from your house in order to get out denotes that you could find yourself feeling rather tired from overwork, but if you clear the snow quickly, then you will be happy in the end.

## Swimming

As long as you are swimming happily in your dream, then success will be yours, but if you are having difficulties this indicates that you have a little treachery going on around you and will be faced with frustrations.

## A Tap

To dream that your water-tap is running constantly is an extremely good indication that your finances are going to be trouble-free.

## Tar

To be able to see tar on a road or smell tar distinctly is indicative of good health, but if it is on the soles of your feet or your clothes, this means that you are going to be taking a journey.

## A Taxi

If you dream of looking for a taxi and getting agitated

because you cannot find one, this indicates that someone is telling you lies. If, on the other hand, you get your taxi easily in the dream and are speeding toward your destination, you can expect a very pleasing letter quickly.

## Tea

To dream that you are enjoying a good cup of tea denotes that you are going to need a little more perseverance in order to achieve your ends.

## Tears

This is a dream image which you can interpret prophetically in reverse because it means a great deal of happiness is coming your way.

## Teeth

To dream of teeth is not a good sign, for it is a warning that you may not be feeling 100 percent fit.

## The Theater

To dream of anything to do with the theater tells you in other words to be rather careful both about your spending and to whom you give your confidences.

## The Throat

To dream that your throat is causing you slight trouble is considered to be quite lucky; the quicker you are able to clear your throat, the quicker the success you are likely to gain.

## A Ticket

To dream that you either buy or are given a ticket for something means that you'll have good news of something about which you have been depressed of late.

### A Tin

While not a good dream image, for it means false friends, if the tin you see in a dream is smooth and not jagged, then you will surmount deceit around you.

### Tiredness

To dream of tiredness is a warning for you to take more rest; otherwise, you could lose ground in your working life.

### Toast

To dream of toast is extremely fortunate, especially where domestic affairs are concerned.

### Toys

To dream of toys indicates to you that one of your family is going to be successful in a test or examination.

### A Triangle

To dream of a triangle means that you are going to be confused either by which of two opportunities to take or by which of two people around you you would rather be with permanently.

### Trousers

To dream of trousers indicates a great deal of fun in a fickle manner, but, if you are not married, this is a slight warning that you could have an argument with someone you love.

### Ugliness

To dream that you are talking with a very ugly person is considered to be extremely fortunate.

### An Umbrella

To dream that you are using an umbrella, and that it is open, is lucky; you will come out of the rain and into the sunshine.

### To Undress

While to dream that you are naked is a fortunate dream, to dream of being undressed in front of others is not so good, for it means scandal or chatter and yourself on the receiving end of unhappiness.

### Unhappiness

Another very fortunate dream; if you are unhappy in a dream, this indicates that you are being wisely cautious and that good luck should predominate for you for quite a while.

### A Uniform

To dream that you see someone in uniform, or that you yourself are wearing a uniform, means that someone around you thinks dearly of you and that you will have great peace and happiness in your domestic life.

### Unkindness

To dream that you yourself are unkind or that someone else is unkind to you is an indication of how loyal and sincere the person of your choice is toward you.

### An Upheaval

To dream that you are in the midst of an upheaval indicates that you are going to reach a very difficult conclusion, which should make you happy after a long period of indecision.

### A Van

To dream of a van means that you are being a little impatient and indicates that, if you are prepared to be patient and persevere, things will eventually come out the way you want them to.

### A Vase

This image in a dream indicates that you are being rather vain and too egotistical and would do better to be more thoughtful of others.

### A Veil

It is never thought to be good to see yourself wearing a veil in a dream, for it is indicative of worry and sadness.

### Vexation

To dream that you are extremely vexed with someone around you, or with the way things are going, denotes great good fortune and pleasing headway for you.

### A Victory

To dream of victory is a warning; it advises you not to get involved in arguments nor to take other people's sides in their personal quarrels.

### A Village

To dream that you see yourself in a beautiful village or a strange village usually indicates a change of work or a change of your position.

### A Vine

To dream of a vine in full fruit means that success is about to come your way, after a lot of hard work.

### A Violin

To dream of a violin being played with a beautiful melody coming from it indicates that you are going to be extremely popular with most people around you. However, should one of the strings break, in the dream, then you may find yourself being the peacemaker of a quarrel.

### A Vision

To see a visionlike representation of a person you know in a dream could be indicative that he is either in slight trouble or will be in the near future.

### Voices

To dream that you can hear a lot of people talking, even if they are happy, is not good, because it indicates holdups and frustrations, especially where your working life is concerned.

### Voting

To dream that you are casting a vote means that you are lacking in confidence and that you have got to put your best foot forward in order to achieve your ambitions.

### Wafting

To dream that you are wafting in the air indicates that you are going to need all your concentration in order to avoid a few annoyances.

### Wages

To dream that you are receiving your wages indicates that there is someone dishonest around you.

### Waistband

To dream that someone is either measuring your waist

or putting a belt on you is extremely fortunate, for it means that you will be receiving some money you had not expected.

## Walking

This dream symbol is indicative of irritations, but if you are striding out energetically, then this tells you that you will get over them with time.

## A Wallet

A wallet in a dream means either an unexpected letter or news of an opportunity coming your way.

## Waltzing

To dream that you are waltzing denotes that you must give a little more encouragement to someone of the opposite sex who is extremely fond of you but a little shy about stating his feelings.

## War

To dream of war is not good because it portends slight dangers ahead for you.

## Washing

To dream you are washing or laundering means slight unrest in your household.

## Wax

To dream of wax is a warning that you are being over-extravagant and should economize more for the moment, otherwise you are going to be worried about your finances.

## A Web

To dream of a web is good, for it usually indicates that you are going to attain most of your wishes.

## Weeping

If you are weeping in a dream, or trying to soothe someone who is weeping, then this indicates a great deal of happiness ahead for you.

## Whistling

To hear whistling in a dream, whether you are the whistler or not, is bad, for it means that someone is talking maliciously about you.

## A Wig

To dream of a wig means a slight indecision lies ahead concerning which of two people you prefer in your love life.

## A Will

To dream that you are reading or making a will indicates happiness and extremely good health for you.

## Wind

To dream that you can hear the wind howling is quite good, for it means great happiness and good fortune for you in the near future.

## Wine

To dream of wine indicates a happy domestic situation for you.

## Winter

To dream of winter and the cold, especially if there is snow to be seen in your dream, means success.

## A Witch

To dream of a witch is considered to be extremely unlucky.

## Yarn

To dream of yarn means that good news or an unexpected gift should be coming to you.

## Yawning

To dream that you are yawning constantly means that you are not giving sufficient attention to details around you, and could be sorry if you do not concentrate a little more.

## Yeast

To dream that you are mixing yeast means that, while financially you will be doing well, you are, nevertheless, at the moment being rather overconfident.

## Yellow

To dream of the color yellow is not good, because it denotes jealousy around you.

## A Yolk

If you are a gambler, to dream of the yolks of eggs is a lucky sign, for it means that you are in a winning period. If you are not a gambler, then this is considered to be a generally fortunate dream.

## A Yule Log

To dream of a yule log denotes that you are going to have great peace of mind, and, if you are single, then you could well be announcing your engagement in the near future.

## A Zipper

To dream that you are dressing in a hurry and that a zipper on your clothing works freely means good news is to come in the near future, but should your zipper be difficult, or stick, this indicates obstacles which you will have to overcome.

## Zircon

To dream of a zircon, which is usually a brownish gem, is not considered to be lucky, for it warns you of deceit around you and of holdups in your plans.

## The Zodiac

To dream that you are studying the signs of the Zodiac indicates that you will prosper greatly through your concentration and learning.

## A Zoo

To dream that you are visiting a zoo is considered to be extremely good, provided that you are not attacked by one of the animals in the dream.

# Chapter IV

# ★ PHRENOLOGY ★

Phrenology is a science of the mind, the brain, within which those telling dreams just described take place. From the shape of the head itself we can tell a fair amount about a person, and, therefore, his future. Let me say here that the brain is something more than a sponge whose job it is to temper the heat of the heart.

Professor Gall, in 1796 in Vienna, gave a series of lectures, trying to show that one could break up the pure entity of the brain into different faculties; one could find these separately within the brain, he maintained. He was, of course, making a study of cerebral physiology, and he was, also of course, ridiculed for this, because he dared to couple the word instinct with physiology. But he was right.

My belief is that human beings and animals possess intellectual capacities in varying degrees, for the mind includes all functions that involve any degree of consciousness. For example, I am at the moment writing this chapter and therefore have a pen in my hand; quite naturally, I am thinking of phrenology when I write, which is of course an action of the mind. At the same time, I am holding my pen between by thumb and fingers in order to shape the letters—in the phrenological sense, these movements are operations which involve mental action, too, because, even though I am grasping the pen which is a mechanical action of the muscles, the muscles are obeying the mandate of my mind. This applies to every other case of voluntary action from any other part of the body.

Every feeling of which we are made conscious involves cerebral action; even though excitement may come from without, its existence in you comes from brain action.

If you were to cut or injure or stop the function of a nerve trunk, you would have destroyed voluntary *motion* where that limb is concerned only. The brain is more necessary to sensation in any part of your body than that part of the body itself; during the last war, many men who had lost a leg, hand or an arm felt pain in that leg, hand or arm *later*. Blind people can see while they are dreaming. We all *see* this way when sleeping, even though our eyes are closed.

When one mentions the word phrenology, one immediately thinks of the head and the bumps that one can feel there. I have often heard this referred to as "bump reading," but in truth there *is* a lot one can learn from the head itself. One can *sectionalize* a person's head and gain an indication from the impressions or depressions of each section of how one could expect that character to behave in different areas.

For example, let us take the first section. On the forehead, just above the eye, you will sometimes see more protrusion in some people than in others; this tells us whether or not a person has got a sense of proportion that is well balanced. Looking at the profile of a head, draw a line straight down, starting at the top in the center of the head to just in front of the ear; halfway between the top of the head and the top of the ear, you'll find a section which tells whether the person is a forward or retiring type, for here most people have, to the experienced fingertip, a slight bump. If it is pronounced, then you can know that this person would like things done in a high and grand manner, but if the bump is not particularly noticeable, then he is probably satisfied with himself and will be more on the retiring side.

Now let us take an area just a little higher than the nape of the neck, but slightly in toward the ear; if a pronounced bump is here, then you know that you have someone who is very affectionate and above average in his sexual desires. Above this, you will quite often get a bump, especially if the person is extremely friendly, and you will know immediately that there you have someone who enjoys other people's company and does not like to be left too much on his own.

Looking at the profile again, you will find that someone who can concentrate well and is methodical by nature possesses a bump just above the ear to the right. If you are able to feel a bump that extends over a good area immediately above the ear, at the side of the head, then you will know that this person has terrific energy, and, where business is concerned, the capability to become a top executive.

Again, looking at the profile of the person where you have drawn your line, proceed halfway down vertically from the very top of the head along the side of the face; if you can feel a bump there, then you know that you have an extremely kind and sympathetic person who will help sensibly and give guidance. Almost next to this, toward the front of the head, another bump would tell you that this person is also very generous and charitable by nature.

Now look immediately above the eyebrow and you should be able to find three slight bumps, although this will be more pronounced in some people than others. The one nearest to the bridge of the nose tells us that this person will be awfully good at evaluations and could even have a keen sense of distance and the weights of things. The second one, halfway across the eyebrow, is indicative of the person's color sense. If this is pronounced, then he will rarely be wrong where his sense of color is concerned. The bump that you can sometimes feel toward the end of the eyebrow, nearest the ear, is the bump that I call the methodical one; when this is pronounced, you would know that if this person works out a method for doing any particular task, it will be an almost faultless method.

Just behind the ear, in the center, a pronounced bump would tell us that we had someone who likes life and has the instinct to resist illness by possessing just that little extra energy that pulls him through.

If you can feel a bump high on the forehead, just toward the left by the hairline, then you have a very genial person who can be quite bland in his approach to most things.

Halfway between the top of the ear and the eyebrow, a

bump tells us that we have a collector, and someone who likes to acquire the unusual in his life.

I have given you what, from my experience, has proved correct in many cases with reference to phrenology. If you want to try this science, you now have the pointers that you will need to tell you the character of any subject. Of course, you will lace these characteristics together yourself in order to know how your subjects will react in certain circumstances.

Chapter V

# ★ FORETELLING THE
# FUTURE BY DICE ★

Parapsychologists are now studying the possibilities of mind over matter, the effect on material things which you can exert merely by *willing* certain results.

It may be that your subconscious comes into play here, but I am convinced that there can be meaning in the roll of dice, for the future.

Not many people realized that when they threw dice, in the old days, they could have told the future in this manner, but those who did were often superstitious about which days of the week they should or should not try to find out what luck held in store for them by this method. It was generally accepted that a Friday or a Sunday was definitely not a day to throw the dice. Usually, the method involved was to take three dice and shake them well in your hand, or in a box, then throw them out onto a round table; should one of the dice or all of them fall from the table when thrown, this indicated upcoming bad feeling, or even a rather nasty quarrel.

For today, I would suggest, too, that you always add the complete value of three dice when you throw them; for example, if you throw three ones, this becomes three; three sixes automatically become eighteen. I shall now tell you—and my information comes from old charts—what the interpretation of the total numbers of three dice thrown represents.

### Three—

This means either that you are entering into a good period for you or that you can expect an unlooked-for yet pleasing gift.

### Four—

This represents the likelihood that caution is necessary, for you could be dealing with someone who will be rather difficult.

### Five—

You can expect to meet a new person who, with time, should prove to be a great friend, and who will be advantageously in your life for a long period.

### Six—

This warns you to keep your eye on either personal things around you or even some*one* of whom you are fond, because it sometimes means that there is dishonesty nearby.

### Seven—

This number indicates chatter, and that you have someone around you who has a very loose tongue, so be careful to whom you divulge your confidences.

### Eight—

This indicates that you have been either a little wrong in your approach to someone or at fault, and you could be on the receiving end of a reprimand.

### Nine—

This number means a festivity, especially in the romantic field; this could be either a wedding or engagement.

### Ten—

This tells you that you will soon be hearing news of a birth; if you yourself are pregnant at the time of throwing the dice, then the number ten not only tells you that you will have a healthy child, but that it will be a boy.

### Eleven—

This number is never a happy one, for, from experience, it has been proven to indicate that either you or someone close to you will be saddened.

### Twelve—

This number usually means that a cable or express letter or urgent telephone call is coming your way.

### Thirteen—

This indicates depression and worry (but not always necessarily, for it can indicate that you are worrying unduly).

### Fouteen—

For the eligible, this usually means a new romantic interest in your life, while for the married it indicates that your partner will be proud of you for something you have achieved.

### Fifteen—

This warns you not to get involved in a quarrel or thoughtless chatter with people who could involve you in an unfortunate manner.

### Sixteen—

This number usually indicates travel of an enjoyable nature.

## Seventeen—

This is a happy number, indicating that while you are going to be extremely busy, you are at the same time going to be on the move from place to place, and there could be a change of residence for you.

## Eighteen—

This is the luckiest number of all to throw, for it indicates a good financial position ahead, a promotion, happy dividends and great advancement in life for you.

Should you find that, after you throw your dice, one of them lands on top of the other, this usually indicates for a man that he should keep his eyes open for an opportunity which is soon to come his way. For a lady, this could mean an increase in her family.

I have indicated for you here what the dice foretell for you when thrown. I will not absolutely state that these outcomes are to be relied upon, but they have been so played over the centuries, and quite a lot of people in their day have sworn by them; so try this method and have fun.

# Chapter VI

# ✳ NAPOLEON'S
# PREDICTION SPINNER ✳

Closely related to the throwing of dice is a prophetic device used in France years ago. In Napoleon's day, if he wanted to know about future riches, romance or recreation, he had a method which was worked out for him by a great psychic of the time. This was done quite simply: by using a square piece of cardboard with numbers from one to twelve going in a clockwise direction. Napoleon would then close his eyes, and, taking a pencil in his hand, rotate the pencil in circles and plunge it onto the cardboard square. Depending on the number nearest the point on which his pencil had landed, he would determine what he wanted to know about his riches or any upcoming romance, or what lay in store for him in his moments of relaxation.

Below I have listed for you the answers that he got in each of these categories. You will note that I have put these predictions in modern language; the language in which they were originally written, while making the same sense, was indeed rather flowery.

## Riches

1.  EXTRA RESPONSIBILITY should be offered to you in the near future and consequently BUSINESS ACTION will take a very healthy turn with conditions being much more favorable—your LUCK IS IN, provided that you do not attempt to do more than you can ACCOMPLISH.

2.  This is a period in which you will wish at times that you were SIX PEOPLE, you will be kept so BUSY. Do everything you can to try to avoid A SLIGHT SETBACK in a TIE-UP with an associate. You would find it much better to try TALKING IT OVER.

3.  This could be one of the BEST PERIODS that you have experienced for quite SOME TIME, so attend to your NFEDS and start getting your DECKS CLEARED. Through just a little thought, you could find that by giving an ORIGINAL APPROACH to an OLD PROBLEM, the result should be MORE SUCCESSFUL.

4.  The ABSENCE of ANOTHER at business could give you the opportunity to make good use of your INITIA-TIVE in being able to ADAPT YOURSELF to a task in a forthright and very SUCCESSFUL MANNER, which without doubt should prove more than remunerative.

5.  This could very well be an ILLUMINATING PE-RIOD for you. You could inadvertently make your point by refraining from ARGUMENTS with an unreasonable person. Remember to be AMBITIOUS yet at the same time not OVERCONFIDENT, and you could have CON-TROL OF THE SITUATION in double-quick time.

6.  If you would attempt to attend to your PREVIOUS

COMMITMENTS before permitting any EXTRA EX-TRAVAGANCES, you should find that you could win FRESH SUPPORT, after what must have been a rather trying period, and this should supply you with the OPTI-MISM that has been lacking.

7.   The indications are that the INFLUENCES around you are now FAVORABLE and that by a little extra EX-ERTION, you should not only be able to keep an UN-RUFFLED ATMOSPHERE at business, but should be able to GAIN quite pleasantly in the FINANCIAL FIELD.

8.   This is a time during which you could make an IM-PORTANT CHOICE of a new ASSOCIATE and find that he is both MELLOW and EXTREMELY SOCIABLE in disposition. At the same time, don't be too ready to SHOULDER ANOTHER'S RESPONSIBILITIES. Bear in mind that your program is quite FULL ENOUGH already.

9.   Happily, business should settle down to ROUTINE at long last and, in consequence, you should be able to get a BREATHER. Try your best not to ANALYZE things TOO DEEPLY; by refraining from this you should find that the SNAGS you expect may not develop.

10.   This is a period for attempting to SETTLE URGENT MATTERS by making quick decisions. It is just as well that your ENERGY is high, for you will be kept fairly MOBILE, yet in consequence, you should most certainly be able to mix quite a lot of PLEASURE with your BUSI-NESS.

11.   The indications are that you could expect some GOOD material results from PAST EXERTIONS, which you thought had GONE UNNOTICED. Remember that your TRUMP CARD is quite definitely your ability to keep up a good relationship with all types. Your POPU-LARITY should pay off and you should be MORE THAN SATISFIED.

12. A very ENCOURAGING PERIOD is due for you which should prove more than adequate, plus the chance of a little EXTRA in the CASH BOX for you. You may associate BUSINESS with PLEASURE, and this, in consequence, should get you ONE STEP NEARER to a PERSONAL AMBITION.

## Romance

1. REMEMBER that you cannot rush things; try to exercise a little more PATIENCE with a sensitive person around you. DON'T BE IMPULSIVE, for you should find that he thinks very highly of you indeed, and your future days, in consequence, could be FULL OF HAPPINESS.

2. YOU SHOULD BE IN TOP FORM and able to manage a DIFFICULT PERSON around you. Also a close friend could at long last make up his mind and there is little doubt that the DECISION HE WILL ARRIVE AT should more than please you.

3. You should be able to make a decision which could STRENGTHEN a NEWLY FORMED TIE and in consequence feel much more SETTLED than of late. Provided that you avoid GOSSIP or INTRIGUE, GREAT GOOD FORTUNE awaits yourself and a loved one, who has of late been in a rather nervous state.

4. There could be a SLIGHT argument with someone you are very fond of over a CHANGE OF RESIDENCE, and in consequence you may feel that you have been DECEIVED. You would do well to HEED YOUR INTUITION, yet at the same time make certain that you CONTROL YOUR EMOTIONS.

5. The whole outlook regarding a member of the OP-

POSITE SEX should favor most of your arrangements from now on, although the very OBSTINATE ACTION of a person who is GETTING ON IN AGE should anger you with respect to his or her attitude regarding someone you hold most dear.

6.   You would be UNWISE to put too much TRUST IN YOUR JUDGMENT regarding the feelings of a member of the OPPOSITE SEX now, for there is the possibility that he could be deceitful. During the next few months, however, you should MORE THAN EXCEL YOURSELF with some of the HAPPIEST COMPANY you have been in for some time past.

7.   Now is a time when you can THROW AWAY YOUR CARES, for more HARMONIOUS RELATION-SHIPS can be expected for you all round. Your opposite number should be extremely delighted by being able to make a DOMESTIC SAVING which should also MORE THAN PLEASE YOU.

8.   Life takes on a much more ROSY HUE FOR YOU, and ROMANCE should without doubt be VERY MUCH IN THE FORE. With just a little patience, you should find that you can go ahead in this area in most directions VERY RAPIDLY INDEED.

9.   You would be well advised to try giving a little MORE ATTENTION to SMALL PERSONAL THINGS with regard to someone of whom you are very fond, and do remember that JEALOUSY can be a VERY BAD FOE—why not relax and show a little more TRUST IN THOSE YOU LOVE.

10.   You should, by using DIPLOMACY, be able to PATCH UP A DISPUTE of some standing with a close friend, and if trying to advance your point, would be advised to use your EVENINGS ROMANTICALLY but TACTFULLY. Indications now suggest that, providing you follow these pointers, you CANNOT GO WRONG.

11.   NOW IS A TIME when you may find that you could quite easily COMMIT yourself ROMANTICALLY, even though a person who is close to you may be rather DIFFICULT TO PLEASE. Provided that you are sure, then be ADAMANT, and with little doubt all should turn out very well indeed.

12.   There could be a LITTLE WORRY for you concerning an individual who stands very close to you. Where ROMANCE is concerned, much better for you to FOLLOW YOUR OWN FEELINGS, as opposed to being guided by a member of your circle, and before very long your HORIZON SHOULD CLEAR and you should be feeling much HAPPIER.

## Recreation

1.   This is an excellent period for making PERSONAL CHANGES; you should find that you GO PLACES and DO THINGS in company that you enjoy to the fullest, so take advantage of the opportunity of being able to turn on your SOCIAL CHARM.

2.   You have a VERY FULL time ahead of you, and yet it would be wrong for you to RELY too much on all the plans you have in mind being fulfilled, because your DOMESTIC PROBLEMS could be under a slight cloud; do not ASSERT your AUTHORITY too much in the home.

3.   You could find that to make the very best use of your TIME FOR RECREATION it would be a good thing to try planning a FUTURE TRIP, which could prove not only happy, but at the same time extremely PROSPEROUS for you. EVENINGS also appear to be the best time of the day for you.

4. There is a strong possibility of your COMPLETING a domestic task to your SATISFACTION; this should put you in FINE FETTLE with your family. Preparation for a FUTURE JOURNEY could, however, take up quite a LARGE SLICE of your time for the moment.

5. You would do well to take things as EASILY as you can FOR THE MOMENT, for you are more TIRED than you might think, and although you have a very BRIGHT time ahead of you and plenty of OPPORTUNITIES FOR ENJOYMENT, it would be wrong to ask too much of it.

6. You are in an ALL-ROUND SPLENDID period and you should be able to complete a LEISURE-TIME TASK to your satisfaction. Your HAPPY-GO-LUCKY attitude plus your CHARM should help you to NET an almost faultless and most enjoyable time.

7. The indications are that you will FULFILL an INVITATION that you had POSTPONED, and thoroughly enjoy yourself. Also, a PERSONAL PLAN could succeed very well by your using tact, yet at the same time you may find that you need ALL YOUR PATIENCE with someone near to you.

8. An ELDERLY PERSON could assist you to carry out a PERSONAL AMBITION of yours; also a SMALL WIN through a GAMBLE should delight you. Keep your eyes open and you should find that you meet a new and very ATTRACTIVE PERSONALITY, and this association could prove to be MUCH LESS OF A DRAIN on your pocket.

9. By BEING INDECISIVE now, you could lose quite a lot of ground in a personal matter. It will be much better for you to HEED THE ADVICE of an older person, especially if MONEY IS CONCERNED, for QUICK ACTION is necessary and his experience INVALUABLE.

10. A very great highlight for you could be a SURPRISE

OUTING, resulting in a REUNION with someone you love, but take care that your past omission to keep a PROMISE, by having been FORGETFUL, does not land you in HOT WATER.

11.   There is very little RELAXATION for you at the moment, for irritating little tasks have to be CLEARED UP, but even so your FORM could not be better, and in consequence you should be GAY and CAREFREE and spend a VERY HAPPY, relaxing period later.

12.   There could be a few difficult and EMBARRASSING moments for you ahead, but MAINTAIN your PATIENCE. This is a period for a SMALL GAMBLE; your luck appears to be FAIRLY GOOD and there is a chance that you should be able to RECOUP PAST LOSSES.

## Chapter VII

# ✦ CARTOMANCY: A GUIDE
## TO READING CARDS ✦

Similar to Napoleon's guide but perhaps more suited in
ways to some today is cartomancy. The science of foretelling the future by using a pack of cards has been handed
down through centuries. There have been a number of
people, well-known and otherwise, who have criticized
this, but I believe there is a good deal to this "game." Nobody appears to know the origin of cartomancy, but there
is little doubt that it has been preserved by gypsies
throughout the ages, and that the country from which it
originally derived was Ancient Egypt. (Some believe that
this way of looking into the future dated back beyond
Egypt to the early Hindus, that it came to Egypt when
certain Hindus migrated west.)

I can only set out for you what in my opinion and from
my experience are the best interpretations for divining the
future by means of playing cards. One point I would like
to make very clear here is that cartomancy is only a *me-
dium* through which a psychic person can work to obtain
his best results; it is not a good thing for amateurs to try
this on total strangers and could be dangerous should one
try to do so. If you will just look on this as a way of foretelling the future for yourself, which does have, as most
human endeavors do, a margin of error, then you should
find that you will have a lot of fun with cards, as well as
be amazed by the number of "hits."

Although I have explained the *method* of cartomancy in
a previous book, I want herewith to give you the meanings

of the fifty-two cards in the pack again, because I feel this book would be incomplete without them. It is up to you to relate these meanings in any one layout of cards.

## Hearts

Hearts are the luckiest suit in the whole pack.

The ACE means a house or residence of some sort.

TWO—A cable or telephone call or something that arrives very quickly.

FOUR—A crossing of water specifically, although all fours, regardless of suit, mean changes of some kind.

You will note that I have left out Hearts Three at this stage, because it is only important when it is found in conjunction with something else, when it means "going."

FIVE—Stands for the initial "E" or can mean a time limit of five (five days, five weeks, five months, etc.).

SIX—The same as Three.

SEVEN—The initial "G" or "J" (which have approximately the same sound).

EIGHT—Needs careful interpreting. It means flirtation with the opposite sex, and the initial "H."

NINE—Is the most important card in the whole pack. It is the "wish" card.

TEN—(Together with all the other tens, regardless of suit) means work, business, government, security or anything that is strong.

The JACK, QUEEN and KING stand for various people; the JACK is a young man with gray eyes, the QUEEN is a woman of the same coloring, and the KING, a man above the age of thirty-five. On occasion, the KING placed next to the JACK means that the young man is going to receive exceptionally good news.

## Diamonds

The ACE means money.

TWO—The initial "B."

THREE—Sometimes the number of days or weeks.

FOUR—A change, which is a good change because it is a red four.

FIVE—Sometimes a little unlucky or indicating some uncertainty.

SIX or SEVEN—Not important.

EIGHT—Indicates some deception.

NINE—The second best card in the pack—another "wish" card.

TEN—Again a security card.

JACK and QUEEN are people with very blue eyes.

KING—Means a doctor or something medical.

## Clubs

ACE—Nighttime. That is any time from noon onward.

TWO—A matter of two months.

THREE—Unimportant.

FOUR—A change for good or bad of some kind.

FIVE—The out-of-town card.

SIX—The initials "F" or "P" (phonetically these are the same, and it is therefore difficult to differentiate).

SEVEN—A gift.

EIGHT—Unimportant.

NINE—Extreme anger.

TEN—Business.
JACK, QUEEN and KING—People with brown or hazel
  eyes.

## Spades

ACE—The unlucky card—the right side up indicates sick-
  ness. Upside down indicates a death.
TWO—A letter or a contract or agreement.
THREE—Anything that is done in a rush.
FOUR—A change for good or ill of some kind.
FIVE—The worry card.
SIX or SEVEN—If with the Ten of Diamonds, indicates
  adultery.
EIGHT—The initial "H."
NINE—Indicates deep depression.
TEN—Is a tough business card.
JACK and QUEEN—Black- or green-eyed people. (The
  Queen can sometimes indicate a widow or divorcee.)
KING—A dentist or a visit to the dentist.

A variation of reading from the cards is to ask your sit
ter to shuffle the pack of cards and cut them into three
packs. You then lay these separate packs face upward on
the table, making three rows one upon the other. Next you
ask your sitter what his birthdate is; for example, if his
birthdate is the 24th of June, 1960, you add this up as follows:
  $2+4+6+1+9+6+0 = 28.$
  Then: $2+8 = 10$
Thus 10 becomes your sitter's birth number. (This involves some numerology: see next chapter.) Commencing
from the left to the right with your three rows of playing
cards, you count every tenth card and give your reading
by stressing the significance of these tenth cards.

# Chapter VIII

# ✳ NUMEROLOGY ✳

We have just been looking at devices for foretelling the future involving numbers. The most advanced study in this area developed into a philosophy called numerology. Many people find this as exact a method of determining one's characteristics and future trends as astrology.

This is how it works. All people fall into one of nine different groups (one of the nine basic numbers—from one to nine) which are governed by the date of their birth.

Let us say that you were born on March 1st. You would then add 3 plus 1 together (March being the third month; thus your 3, and of course, the one comes from the day of your birth being the first). To this, you add all the separate numbers of the year of your birth. If the total comes to more than 9, then add *these* numbers together again, and your number group is the *sum* of these, so that if by adding your birthday, month and year together, the number came to 25, then, since 2 plus 5 makes 7, your number group would be 7. Two specific examples should put the record straight.

You were born on April 2nd, 1916. Therefore: 2 + 4, April being the fourth month of the year, plus 1 + 9 + 1 + 6 = 23. Now, add 2 and 3 and this gives you your group—5.

Again, say you were born on June 2, 1910. Therefore; 2 + 6 + 1 + 9 + 1 + 0 = 19. Now add 1 and 9, making 10. So we go further here and, finally: 1 + 0 = 1, which is your group.

Having got your number, study this guide to your main characteristics:

1.  You have more common sense than imagination. You are a serious, conscientious, often ready worker. These attributes are nearly always combined with a dash of originality.

2.  You are fairly cool at times and quite deliberate. You possess good sense and discrimination. Quite often you are conventional, disliking changes, loving form and beauty. You are very rarely mean, but sometimes a little too economical.

3.  You can sometimes be mixed up. On the one hand, charming and intuitive; on the other hand, you possess the faculty for making others feel unwelcome when you are in a mood. You do not suffer fools gladly, and rarely are you insistent in your emotions or your policies. People who have the birth number 3 need to choose strong life partners.

4.  You are pioneer go-getters; a little dogmatic and possessive on occasion, but also generous and courageous. You do not change your minds easily and you make good friends.

5.  While you are extremely hospitable, you are luxury-loving, and quick-tempered, yet, at the same time, equally quick to forgive. You believe in helping others, but unfortunately there are times when you get let down yourselves.

6.  You can be stubborn, head-in-the-sand types at times; usually your choice of a partner surprises even your closest friends or relatives.

7.  Artistic, idealistic, yet with a good business head, you possess a vivid imagination and have a changeable nature so that people can often expect you to be moody.

8.  You are proud and discriminating in your choice of

friends. You are most successful and ambitious, but at times you have a fault of being inclined to self-righteousness.

9.   You are usually tidy, neat and fastidious, often to the point of fussiness in the home. You are very loyal and extremely efficient at work. You're often of great help when needed, always provided that you consider the recipient worthy.

# Chapter IX

## ✶ PALMISTRY ✶

Another old, established method for divining what lies in store is palmistry. It can be as exacting as numerology. Many people scoff at even the possibility of foreseeing future events in such a manner. I find that I often get quite a kick out of surprising the confirmed unbeliever with my gift here.

One such opportunity came when I was attending a party at Joan Cohn's house in Beverly Hills. Joan is the widow of the late Harry Cohn, the man who founded Columbia Films. A man whom I had never seen before in my life, but who was a fellow guest brought along by somebody else, slipped and injured his hand. I was bandaging it when he said, "The others tell me that you are pretty good at foretelling the future. Do you read palms? If so, now that you are bandaging my hand, what can you see in my palm?"

"Well," I replied, "the most immediate news that I can give you is that you are, I think, an architect by profession, and that you are going to get a very big contract soon, and even though you will laugh, I can tell you that you are only going to get it by playing golf."

"Now come along, Maurice," he said. "I've never played golf in my entire life, and I'm not even thinking of starting now."

This man's name was Don Hensman; he is one of the foremost architects in California and has designed many beautiful houses for the stars and others in Beverly Hills and Palm Springs, although I did not know this at the time. Some ten days later, he telephoned me at my apartment in Beverly Hills.

He said, "You know, you're quite a frightening man, Maurice. I hate to admit it, but you were right. You mentioned the possibility of a big contract, and even though I said I wouldn't, I have taken up golf and, in consequence, have landed the job. The man with whom I was trying to do business is a mad golf enthusiast, and the only place I could nail him down to talk was on the golf course, so now I am a golf bore—and I've got you to thank for it!"

Now and again, I have to tell people some curious things. A couple of years ago, I met a beautiful girl, and I automatically knew she was an actress; as many do, she then said to me: "Tell me what is going to happen to me." I asked her what her birth sign was, and she told me she was a Taurian; then, more for fun than anything else, I looked at her palm. (Basically, I am not a palmist, although I have great respect for this art.) I told this lady that, in my opinion, she would meet and marry a man who was not English, who would have an initial "P," that she would have to live in two homes, one across the water, and that she would meet opposition to her marriage. I also saw that she had an extremely strong fate line in her hand, so that her career would go quite well; she was in fact likely to become stronger, and, in doing so, change slightly. Because of this, she would meet up with slight jealousy, I foresaw, but I added that she had no need to worry about this.

My lady consultant turned out to be Susan Hampshire, and I got an extremely pleasant surprise on picking up a magazine one day and reading just these words, written by Susan.

"I had a reading with Maurice Woodruff once. He was incredible. It was before I met my husband, Pierre, and Maurice said: You are going to meet somebody, or have met somebody who is dark, who speaks another language. You will travel across water, you will have two homes in two different lands, you will marry this man, but nobody wants you to marry. The marriage will be a great success, and there will ultimately be three children. He will have much more money than he tells you he's got. I didn't tell Pierre that for the first eighteen months. I thought I'd keep it up my sleeve. It's quite extraordinary, isn't it? He said that I would do something that would change my working life, which has obviously been *The Saga,* that I would go into it, that I would be rather pushed around a bit, that I would be quite jealous of someone in it, that it would be all right in the end. All of which has proved to be quite true."

When I was only about six or seven years of age, my mother, who was one of the most famous clairvoyants of her time (among her clients was the Duchess of Windsor), took me to see a very well-known palmist. His name was Cheiro, and at the time I was taken to see him, he was the rage of Edwardian society, for he had read the hands of such immortals as the famous Mark Twain. While I do not remember what he said, my mother told me a story about him which I never forgot. Evidently, on one occasion, a leading society lady took Cheiro, by arrangement, to read the palm of an extremely famous person. She insisted that he must not see this person's face. She herself took Cheiro into a room and sat him by a table in front of closed curtains.

Suddenly, a hand was thrust between the folds of the curtains, and, thoroughly baffled, this famous palmist proceeded to up-turned palms. It was not until years later that he discovered that he had been reading the hands of King Edward VII.

I tell you this story in order to show you that "looking into the future" by any known method is something that intrigues the highest in the land just as much as the holidaymaker who will gaze anxiously (or skeptically) into the face of a dark-haired gypsy who is looking into a crystal ball.

Make no mistake, "looking into the future" is booming throughout the world as never before. I know from experience. I have so many clients on my books right now that I am already having to make appointments well into next year. You may well ask, why this boom? My feeling is that the fact that life moves so fast these days breeds a greater sense of insecurity than ever before. People want to know what lies in store for them, and science has made such great strides in so many directions that people generally all over the world are becoming convinced that anything is possible—even foretelling the future. And, more and more, ESP, in particular, and science are joining hands.

In order to look into anybody's future by palmistry, you should remember that you must consult his *right* hand. The *left* hand denotes the characteristics that a person was born with and the lines on it generally remain immutable.

Sometimes, the lines on the right hand will change or even disappear altogether. The reason for this is that these lines denote what you have already made of life as well as giving indications of what you are likely to do in the future. For example, a very dear friend of mine was Alma Cogan; in reading her hand, I noted by the slope of her fingers that these indicated a musical person who should find success. Both her hand and heart lines were of very good length and impression which immediately suggested to me a person who would be extremely loyal to someone whom she liked, but would not allow her heart to run away with her head; the only line that came to a sudden termination was her life line, which while it did not indicate the cause of her death, most strongly suggested that she would not be long-lived. Unfortunately, she died at thirty-four.

The lines on your right hand will alter or even disappear, however, so that should you see a hand that has what appears to be a short life line, this does not necessarily mean that the person will die at a young age; quite often, I have seen short life lines, but on further examination have noticed that a little farther along, the line recommences. This could denote that there could be either a slight sickness upcoming or that at the particular time that one sees the gap, the person could be at a rather low ebb.

Another most interesting hand at which I looked was that of Viscountess Tarbat, who is a fashion expert and teacher of deportment for debutantes. Her hand was very artistic, yet at the same time a working hand. I noticed that when she held her hand up to show it, the fingers were held close together, which indicates caution. Her fate line ran into the life line. This indicated that she had at one time taken a very big decision. I looked at her marriage line and saw one strong line branching from it, which told me that she had one child. Here, my clairvoyant gift came into play, and I said that this child was a boy and that her decision had been taken on this boy's behalf; all of this proved to be true, for she afterward told me that she had decided to take up an artistic profession in order to give her boy a good chance and future. At the same time, I told her from the general look of her hand that her judgment was shrewd and could be relied on because, when the fate line ran into the life line, it indicated to me the ability to supervise other people. It was at this stage that she told me that she was teaching debutantes deportment.

On the following chart, I have tried my best to show all the most important lines on the right-hand palm, but remember that not every hand will carry a complete set so do not get worried or surprised if you cannot find some of these lines on yours or someone else's palm, for a "complete" hand is very rare indeed. Here is what each line that you will see means.

## The Fate Line:

This is sometimes known as the Line of Saturn, and it usually denotes to the palmist just how that person's chosen work or career should shape up and how much success (or even how many setbacks) can be expected. Remember that any breaks or weaknesses in this line all have their importance. A strong fate line which increases in strength as it goes along will indicate that its owner should go well ahead to success on whichever path he has chosen in business.

## The Success Line:

Here we have a line that is not found on every hand that you will see; it appears to have no laid-down starting point or length. Thus, whenever you see it clearly and strongly marked, it indicates very good capabilities which should lead to success; the length of the line indicates in

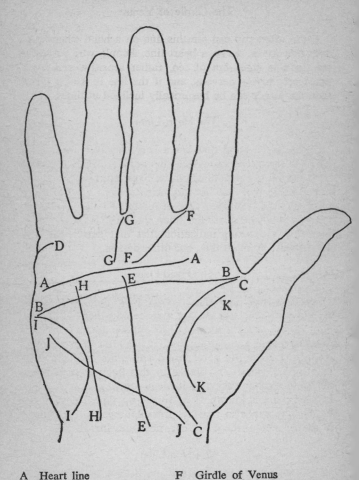

| | | | |
|---|---|---|---|
| A | Heart line | F | Girdle of Venus |
| B | Head line | G | Intuition line |
| C | Life line | H | Line of Success |
| D | Marriage line | I | Another line of intuition |
| E | Fate line | J | Line of health |

K  Line of influence

turn the greatness of the success and its period of duration.

### The Girdle of Venus:

Quite often you can see this line on a hand where there does not appear to be a heart line. People who possess it are, in nine cases out of ten, rather sensitive and sometimes very highly nervous, and if the line is thin in places then the owner can be hysterically inclined at times.

### The Heart Line:

If you see a hand that has a very clearly marked heart line, then you will know that this person usually has deep affection for the people whom he likes. He can at times be rather dogmatic, but is very kind. Such a person can nearly always take good care of himself should a crisis develop. Should little branch lines shoot off from the heart line, this is a strong indication that that person can give out affection to more than one other person.

### The Head Line:

A good head line should start with the life line and should run fairly straight for a space and then slope away very slightly toward the wrist. If you see a clearly marked head line, then you can know that the owner possesses not only good sense but good vision and quite excellent judgment. When there are breaks in this line, or even weaknesses in the impression of it, then you have a person who is often what is known as a "mixed-up type." Weaknesses in the line can also indicate irregular health, particularly in the regions of the head, ear, nose and throat.

### Intuition Line:

This is another line that may not be seen on every hand, so do not worry if you do not see it on your own. It can indicate a keen mind. I saw this very clearly indicated on Liberace's palm and pointed it out to Lee, as he is known to his friends. I was able to tell him that this shows that his determination, when he feels that he is doing the correct thing regarding this work, proves to be more often right than wrong. People who possess this line on their hands will be dogmatic in their opinions of events and also of people, and they are not usually proved wrong. An interesting point here is that psychic people nearly always have this line on their hands.

### The Life Line:

For you to know that you'll have a long and healthy life, this line should be deep, clear and well cut on your palm. As I have said before, do not be worried if it weakens in parts. This just indicates sickness or little ailments at those times; if you possess a hand that has a fairly clear line up to a certain point, then comes to a stop, but continues again even weakly, remember it is the continuance of this line and its length that denotes your span.

### The Influence Line:

When you are able to see this line on someone's hand —and it isn't always there—then it usually means that the constitution of this person is fairly strong. If this is accompanied by a strong life line, then it is indeed an excellent line to possess. The long-lived, the vital people and the battlers of life nearly always have it.

### The Health Line:

This is a line that does invariably leave you with time. It is not often seen, in fact, after sixteen years of age. If it is seen later, it usually belongs to the people who "live it up" in this world. At the same time, if this line accompanies a very good head line, then it also means both a strong constitution and an extremely good memory.

### The Marriage Line:

It is quite usual to be able to tell, according to the depth and the clearness of this line (and, naturally, it is not always seen), the depth of a person's affections; the branches leading off from it denote the number of offspring that can be expected from a marriage. If you find that your marriage line branches into two lines, sloping away from each other, then this indicates either a second romance or a second marriage.

I have tried here to give you the fundamentals of the palmist's profession. You will, of course, realize that a great deal must depend on practice, and on your own skill in the interpretation of the prints that nature has given you. Application of a little elementary psychology can also help.

# Chapter X

# ⋆ HANDWRITING ⋆

Also concerned with trends, but quite different from palmistry is graphology, or the art of being able to read character from handwriting. This has become more accepted, even among professional people, as the years have gone by. I well remember, a few years ago, doing a television program and having the honor of meeting Miss Mercia Cambridge, who had at times been called in by police to read the writing of suspects; she, in my opinon, was quite brilliant in this field.

Graphology is considered by many psychologists to be in the forefront where the study of personality is concerned; the reliability of the handwriting analyst has been proven correct time and time again. I would like to make it clear from the start that quite naturally people's handwriting in almost all cases develops from childhood to middle age, commencing with the child's scribble. As we all know, children love to take a piece of paper and pencil and make lots of lines and patterns; but these lines and patterns begin quite soon. Even from early childhood, I believe that one can see the formation of character here for where one child will make little rings in a light manner, another child will pencil in with heavy thick lines. On the other hand, you will of course get a child who makes rather tensely terminated motions. This goes on until the youngster begins to feel more confident, and then, after a little teaching, he begins to write. Therefore, at an early age, a person begins to write letters and sentences, and w can say that his handwriting is a fairly certain guide to his character even then.

The simplest way to try to "get" a person's character through his handwriting is either to ask him to write a sentence for you or to take a letter that has been written by him. With a ruler, draw a straight line immediately below the first six words. If the words lie fairly evenly along the ruled line, then you know that you are dealing with a person who has a set mind and a fairly even temper. If, on the other hand, you find that the words at times appear to lean down, and don't run straight across the paper, even cutting down through your ruling, then you have someone who either will not see or will lose opportunities from time to time. Should the words run in an opposite manner, in an upward direction, then this person is ambitious but his work will vary at times from good to excellent and back again.

Now take a look at the individual letters. If the writer has good rounded letters, this tells you that he is affectionate by nature and easy to get on with, because of his great friendliness. If you should find that each letter in a word is perfectly formed, then you have a tidy, methodical person who could at times be inclined to fussiness.

Now take a look at the downward strokes of the letters; if these down strokes appear to be heavier than the upward ones, then you will know that your character has a high degree of intelligence but is sensitive and inclined to worry over small things a great deal.

Next, take a look at the joining of the letters. For instance if you have in a sentence the word "are," look and see whether the "A" and the "R" are joined at or near the top of the letters, or whether the joining begins at the bottom, near the line you originally ruled underneath the words. Should they join at the top, then this is not a person I would go to, were I seeking advice. On the other hand, if they are at the bottom, then I would know that I could rely on this person's thoughts and opinions.

Now take a look at the capital letters. If the capitals are separate from the rest of the words, and a little bit inclined to be flamboyant or flowery, then the writer is artistic by nature and also enjoys the good things of life, *and* is an extrovert. On the other hand, if the capital is still un-joined but is well written, then the writer is charitable, easy-going and at times overgenerous. Should the capital, plus the other letters of that word, be completely joined, then you have a person whose feet are firmly on the ground in a practical manner.

Now look at the shape of the person's writing. Where you have good even writing going from left to right in what is regarded as a good commercial hand, then you know that the writer has a good business sense once he has harnessed his abilities. Should the writing slope in a backhanded fashion from right to left, then the writer is artistic and would do better working in a creative field. Where the handwriting appears to be disjointed—for ex-ample, if it starts with a backhanded slope, then becomes slightly upright and irregular—you have a person who has a fairly good brain, but one who is undisciplined and lives on his nerves.

When you find that the overall word appears to be full of flourishes, then you can fairly confidently know that your writer is a good host, that he is kind and comfortable and would welcome you into his home.

It is of the utmost importance when reading character from handwriting that you concentrate on the amount of space the writer takes with his words and on the size of all his letters: as you must be aware, you can have a writer who seems to want to crowd as many words onto his page as possible; therefore his writing necessarily is small, and each word, while tidy, is very close to the others. On the other hand, you may find another writer who scrawls his words and thus fills his page much more quickly. In order to know the difference between a big and a small letter you'll find that a good guide is: if a small letter is two-tenths the size of a capital one in height, it can be consid-ered average. If less, then you can judge it to be short or small. If the small letter is four-tenths of a capital in height, this is considered fairly large, but if taller than four-tenths, then it is considered big. The person who writes and gives good even spacing with both his letters and words, you can judge to possess clarity and a free mind. The person who writes with a good rhythm and whose writing is large (but you can see that he is a quick writer with no breaks in his letters) is in fairly good health and is a pretty energetic character.

On the other hand, when you see small writing, and that the writer has obviously used little pressure on his pen (so that the writing appears to be slightly weak and is not even, but occasionally has abnormal features), then you will know that this writer is either lacking in energy or that his health is not 100 percent.

If you find that the writing in front of you is written similarly to the way you would expect to see the notes on a sheet of music, then you will know that this writer is either a musician or is musically minded.

Where writing appears to have been done rather quickly, and each word does not appear to have any starting stroke, then you will know that the writer is witty and very quick in speech.

When you meet up with large letters with good clarity, but ones that appear to have an individual forming, then you will know that this writer is original in his thoughts and deeds.

When the writing is of a high standard but appears from time to time to be disconnected, this tells you that you have a person with strong intuitive powers.

Full writing, which is flowery, as I have said, comes from an artistic person, yet at the same time it tells you that the writer is gifted with a strong imagination. Most actors and authors possess this type of writing.

When you meet writing in which the writer will here and there omit certain letters or even a word in a sentence, this tells you that the writer is either vague or does not have a good memory, and, according to the meaning of his sentences, it could appear that his mind is either not completely on what he is writing or lapses occasionally, in which case he may be in need of a doctor's care, for mentally he is not functioning as well as he ought.

When you see writing that is neat and small but occasionally has a last-minute addition or alteration, it usually belongs to a very health-conscious person—perhaps a hypochondriac.

When writing is fairly upright all the way through the

sentence, the person is usually a serene, calm character, not easily knocked off balance.

When at the beginning of a sample of writing, the first stroke appears to start below the level of the word (if, for example, the letter is a "T," and the first stroke continues mounting in one line toward the cross of the "T" without a break), then you know that you have a character who will need to be handled, at times, with kid gloves, because he can quite easily be irritated.

When the writing is generally small, and even the capitals appear to be small, then you have an intelligent person, and one who is at the same time not only modest but an introvert.

When you have words written in which it appears that the vertical strokes from the main bases, of the capital "E," say, have extra-heavy pressure and become quite thick at their ends, then the writer is capable of cruelty.

When the capital letters are much larger than the others, yet not decorative or flowery, then you have a person given to boasting a great deal.

When you see writing that slopes more to the left than to the right, and also in which one letter is connected to another by a loop at the top, here you know that you have a person gifted with strong imagination who can at times not tell the truth.

When you get small letters in a word, even apart from the word, and one letter may be much smaller than the others—in other words, stand out as very small—this tells you that the writer can be slightly touchy at times and would be inclined to jealousy.

When you see words that are written quite clearly without having any flowery starts or finishes, or even any strokes to begin words, then you know that you have a person who is very intelligent and can grasp a situation very quickly.

When the writing is large and very regular, and you are able to see that this has been written in a strong hand, here you will realize is a leader, who can either organize or pioneer things.

When writing slants to the right, and the starting and connecting strokes of the letters are fairly large, you will immediately know that you have a good worker, who is earnest about his tasks.

When the end of a word or the end of a sentence appears to be more evenly or regularly written than the start, this means exactly what it implies, that the writer is a person who winds up his job or anything he's doing with great strength.

If you see the letters "A," "F" or "T" and the start or finish curls round to a dot, or even if the crossing of the "F" or "T" finishes with a dot, then you know that you have a fairly tough person to deal with.

Writing that is fairly upright but has been written slowly and with obvious effort (and if the writer has not bothered to space properly or punctuate) indicates that the writer is by nature quite lazy.

When you see writing that does not have signs of stubbornness or irritability, then you will realize the writer can adapt himself and work quite amicably with most people around him.

When the writing flows to the right and is even and very legible, then you have a character who is extremely honest.

When you see writing that is weak, and the strokes are not even but appear to be spidery, then you know that this person is nervous and inclined to drink a little.

When the writer wastes a lot of space, this informs you that he is extravagant and overspends.

When the writer finishes his writing with a flourish underneath a word or signature, then he is inclined to be sexy.

Referring again to capital letters, quite a lot of people print their capital letters and do not "write" them, and these, you can invariably find, are the critics of the world —not always do you hear them talking nicely about others; more often than not, they are analyzing, probably negatively. Also, people who use capitals in this manner live on their nerves.

If, when writing a sentence, a writer crosses his "T" with a long throw-away line, then you would not be far wrong in assuming that this is a person of character, who most certainly lets one know exactly where he stands, because he has definite opinions and definite likes and dislikes.

Should, however, the "T" (and bear in mind that in a sentence a lot of "T"'s are usually used) be crossed in a curly or decorative manner, then the writer either has a few old-fashioned approaches to life or can be rather sensitive about things.

Now let's turn to the letter "E." If the "E" is written in a round circular movement, bearing toward the right, then the writer is efficient and artistic, but should he make his "E" look like the letter 3 back to front, then your writer is very self-satisfied.

When the heights of letters, in forming either a name or a sentence, vary, this usually reveals that the writer is gifted with a strong imagination. Quite a lot of authors write like this.

A person who writes his signature not only with slight flourishes but in an upward direction usually is indicating his versatility here.

The person who signs his name with capitals that emphasize large-sized letters, of good clarity, is extremely proud, but also sensitive to atmospheres or people.

When you see very small writing with no flourishes or great show, then the writer is both quite "human" and possesses modesty.

The person who makes extremely good use of his paper, and writes in an angular manner with no large flowing letters either has the mind of an accountant or an economist

When writing appears to be more upright than usual but is average-sized and fine-lined, then you know that you have an extremely tactful and diplomatic person to dea with.

When you see writing that appears to be rather apathetic or lazy, but which, at times, appears to come to life for just one word or so, then you can know that you have a person who is apt to get depressed frequently but who also lives in his own little world.

I have just given you a few examples of the characteristics that you can determine from a person's handwriting From experience, I have found that the best way to star trying your hand at graphology is to take a letter that yo have received from a friend or relative and place it on a table in front of you. Then pick out any one or two words (the longer the word, the better) which start with a capital letter. Going by the pointers I have already given you, you will be amazed at how quickly you will be able to assess not only the character but the mannerisms of the writer. When you have done this several times, you should then be in a position to judge the letters of strangers. For example, should you receive a business letter, you could rely quite a lot on your judgment of the person's writing to tell you the type of person with whom you are going to have business dealings. Have a go. I am certain that you will gain not only a lot of fun from this, but also quite a degree of knowledge.

# Chapter XI

## ★ SUPERSTITIONS ★

There are some omens from life itself which have stood the test of tradition. (Don't take them too seriously, though.)

It is a good omen for an elderly man or woman to be the first to enter a theater on the first night of a play. Such an occurrence promises a longer run for the play than if a young person should come in first.

It is lucky if, at the last rehearsal, everything goes wrong!

Red sky at night, sailor's delight.

Let a girl hang a wishbone over the door on New Year's Day and the first man who enters will be her husband.

These are a few among many superstitions; I am constantly asked by friends, in business and by readers about all the different superstitions that exist. They want to know how these superstitions originated, whether they should take them as valid or as nonsense, and what I myself accept from them, or reject. They also ask me what the superstitions of various stars or celebrities throughout the world are.

I shall try to list for you here several of the key superstitions that do exist, and give you some thoughts on them. It is interesting that both extremely intelligent as well as average people are, without being aware of the fact, often ruled by occurrences that are superstitions.

In the old days, many of these sayings or beliefs were

frowned upon greatly by the so-called wise, and even by the Church, but they have without doubt lived through the ages, and are still accepted by a large percentage of the public. And many of these *came* from the Church. For example, how often do you hear the expression, "Touch wood," said as an everyday statement? I'm sure that a lot of people who use these two words have no idea why they should be saying "Touch wood." In actual fact, this expression, and the expression "Keep your fingers crossed," derived from religion; "Touch wood" meant touching the cross of Christ, and "Keeping one's fingers crossed" originated again from Christianity, when it was thought that by keeping one's fingers crossed one kept evil at bay.

There are a few examples of celebrities' superstitions:

Julie Andrews never sings a song on the stage until she has broken a piece of bread. She does not know why, but to use her own words, "It's lucky."

Michael Redgrave confesses to having a number of superstitions, his pet one being an aversion to good-natured people coming into his dressing room on a first night before a show to wish him good luck. To use his own words, "It's fatal. I don't mind the good-luck telegrams; they can be opened after the show."

Kirsten Thorborg, the Swedish actress, used to refuse to budge until a member of the cast had kicked her three times.

Superstitions even enter the field of sports. For example, the famous English football manager, Sir Stanley Matthews, borrows boot laces for luck. The test cricketer Bill Edrich makes a point of always putting on his left pad first before going into bat, and a once well-known South African off-brake bowler, Hugh Tayfield, used to kiss his cap before giving it to the umpire before each over, and then before every run up to the wicket he would tap his right foot on the ground. "I've always done it," he said, "it's lucky."

I have known several women who go to whist drives, bridge or bingo sessions, say, and who, when they sit down, pull a lucky coin, a wishbone or a rabbit's foot out of their handbags to place on the scoring card.

I myself have superstitions: I always keep sheaves of wheat in my apartments in both London and America, and in my house in the country, plus an unopened packet of salt in each of these places, for, even though it may seem like an appeasement to the gods, in fact, it is a good old custom. It is said that while you have wheat in your home (which, by the way, if cultivated, can be quite decorative), you will never lack for bread; after all, wheat, when ground, makes bread—and salt is to purify things. (In the old days, they used to rub salt into sailors' backs after they had been thrashed for misdeeds, in order to make certain that their wounds did not turn septic.)

In England, the famous Savoy Hotel Grill Room at one time used to keep a special guest for wedding parties of thirteen. "He" was a magnificently carved black cat in wood, always on such occasions solemnly placed in a chair before a place set for the fourteenth person.

Film star Stephen Boyd was quite firm about his superstition; Stephen told me that he was given, many years ago, a pair of cuff links. The donor wished him luck with them, and now no matter what part he may be playing (even when he was playing in *Ben Hur*), those cuff links are with him on the set on his person. His explanation is that they were given him for luck, that he does not wish to tempt fate, and therefore when doing his work or anything of great importance, he is never going to be without them. (At the time Stephen was making the film *Ben Hur*, I teased him a little about this: "Where on earth have you got your cuff links tucked, Stephen?")

I often meet people who are not stars, of course: a large number of people I know have a superstition about not wearing the color green, or having the color green in their homes. Funnily enough, my manager, Harry Arnold, won't have it, and, on questioning him, I learned that his father would not have this color around him when he was alive. I said to Harry, "The reason you will not have green around you is because it was instilled into you by your father's belief," and his reply was "Quite definitely not. As a matter of fact, I tried to go against my father in this, and defiantly wore a green shirt and a green tie on several occasions over the years, but each time I met with misfortune, and I therefore felt that the point had been proven to me—I have no intention of giving myself bad luck by being stubborn now. I go with this all the way."

As so many people held this superstition about the color green, I decided to look into it to try to find its origin. It makes quite a lot of sense; I found that in the old days evil spirits were represented by the color green, and even today, when you see a Shakespearean play or even a children's play, in more cases than not the wicked fairy or witch is invariably given a green spotlight or a green setting. This was one explanation. The second explanation was that green is the color of mildew, and who, after all, wants a piece of, say, mildewed bread.

My very good friend of years standing, Peter Sellers, told me that he has proven over the years that if he has a ring with either a sapphire in it or a lapis lazuli, good fortune seems to desert him; any job that he may be working on at the time of wearing either of these stones appears to go wrong. Also, he does not like to hear whistling in either his dressing room or on the set when working.

There is an old saying, "The proof of the pudding is in the eating," and over the years, one does prove whether things are fortunate or unfortunate to one's self. It is just a little stupid to continue wearing, doing or hearing certain things if you have proved beyond coincidence that they bode ill for you.

For example, I know a certain piece of music; on every occasion that I have ever heard this, I could almost hear bad luck starting; psychologically, this became a pet aversion of mine. I would not allow a recording of the piece in my house, and if I were in a restaurant or at a ball or any other event when this piece of music was played, I would, if possible, get up and leave at once rather than continue to hear it being played or sung. If I could not do this, I would revert to sitting there unhappily with my fingers crossed under the table (crossed fingers deriving, again, from warding off evil spirits).

Another good friend of mine has what I term a numerology superstition. This is the world-famous racing motorist Stirling Moss. Stirling feels quite genuinely that the number seven it good fortune for him. It appears to have followed him throughout his life. His personal car registration number is M7, his mother was born on the seventh of the seventh month, his sister was born on the twenty-seventh of the month and his beautiful little baby daughter, Allison, was born on the twenty-fifth of December (of course two and five make seven).

The famous English musical comedy actress Millicent Martin, whom you will be seeing often in the near future on your television screens in America, is a very dear friend of mine. She tells me that she doesn't really have any great superstitions either for good or bad. She does occasionally accept certain theatrical feelings, though: for example, she agrees that there should not be live flowers on the stage, for these live flowers are inclined to wither, which could mean that the show might not last very long. She believes firmly in logic and feels that if people do have a pet superstition then of course they must have a reason for it, but she thinks it is dangerous to allow one's self to become obsessed over certain omens. Millicent clearly says that she believes *absolutely* in psychic work, because it has been proven to her on the many occasions when I have given her readings, but this of course does not fall in the realm of superstitions.

Arlene Dahl who, in my opinion, is one of the world's most beautiful women, told me that she didn't really have any special superstitions. She said, when I asked her if she had any, and I quote, "Not really; only the usual ones such as not walking under a ladder. I do have one thing that I don't like which could I suppose be termed as a superstition, and has been said to be an old one—I don't like to have a black cat around me; more especially if I am making a film or doing a show, because I immediately get a feeling that my film or show will not be a success if I see one."

"When you have finished this film, Lionel, you will go on to doing a musical, which should have tremendous success." This is what I said to film star Lionel Jeffries in Hollywood in the early part of 1967, when we were on the set at Warner Brothers, while Lionel was making the film *Camelot*, in which he played the part of the aged king.

(I received a telephone call from Lionel recently in

which he said that I most certainly knew my job well, for he told me that just before he finished *Camelot* in Hollywood, he was sent a script for a musical which he has now completed; this film, currently showing successfully, in which Lionel stars with Sally Ann Howes and Dick Van Dyke, is called *Chitty Chitty Bang Bang*.

I thought I would try to look into the superstition of people not liking to hear quotes from *Macbeth*. I learned that it dates back to the three witches in the play. In the old days, it was apparently considered that their wickedness came through to the hearer and brought in its train bad luck.

Another unusual superstition, which is held by someone I think very highly of indeed, came to me through a man you will see on your television screens, Bruce Forsyth. Bruce is one of the very few stars, I feel, whose feet have remained very much on the ground, as it were, and while most of us know he is a wonderful performer, my feeling is that we have yet to see the tremendous talent of this artist, especially in America. It is my opinion that within the next two years, he will become an international name to be reckond with. You may have seen a small cameo part which he played in Julie Andrews' film, *Star*. I have already told you that a lot of people hold the superstition that they should not have the color green around them. Bruce, on the other hand, doesn't mind having green around him. As a matter of fact, he will even wear green occasionally, but he will not have green candy either in his home or in his dressing room, and, like so many other stars, he tells me that if you want to harass him slightly before a program, then you have only got to whistle in his dressing room or backstage. Also, even should Bruce split a fingernail, he will never file it on a Friday. This superstition goes back to religion, too: as we all know, it was long considered wrong to do anything on a Sunday. All superstitions get embroidered upon as they come down through the years, and the saying developed that one should not file or cut his nails on a Friday or a Sunday (Friday being the day of Christ's crucifixion).

My long-time friend Roger Moore, star of "The Saint" television series and of quite a few Hollywood productions, while he holds quite a few superstitions, never loses his tremendous sense of humor. When I asked Roger what his pet superstition was, he said, "Oh, I never throw salt over my left shoulder when I spill it, because it might catch the man sitting behind me in the eye," but nevertheless, Roger obviously has a feeling about the dropping of salt, as have many others. When I looked into the reason for the dropping of salt (I have already mentioned that salt is in effect a purifier), I found that people once thought that to drop salt was bad luck, because then you drop the thing that kept you pure and chaste. Here again, I suppose Roger does not really want to tempt the fates. He tells me that most other superstitions he tries to prove wrong.

An actress who is also a wonderful singer and a very dear friend of mine (and whose name I predict will be on most people's lips before long) is Anne Rogers. (You may remember she was given the Sarah Siddons Award for her performance in *My Fair Lady* on Broadway and throughout the States.) She tells me that she does not have a pet superstition but is rather scared of anybody telling her of a new superstition, because while she knows most of the well-known ones, she would be frightened of becoming obsessed by any new ones. She feels that she can cope and get along quite nicely with those she has been told about, but might find new ones subconsciously running her life for her. This is an understandable outlook.

Anne's view is shared very strongly by another friend of mine, who is currently starring in London in *Man of La Mancha*, Keith Michell. Keith has made quite a lot of films and starred on Broadway in several productions, including *Irma La Douce*. Keith's words to me on this subject, in his dressing room, were, "I try my best not to believe many superstitions, and may I stress to you, Maurice, I try." Keith is playing the leading role in the musical now, and he is quite brilliant in it, but Don Quixote, the character whom he portrays, was a man full of imagination and superstition; so I would be prepared to wager that it would not be possible for an actor of Keith's caliber to give such a tender and wonderful performance as this without in some way becoming at least subconsciously somewhat superstitious.

What other common superstitions do we have? While many of you may know them, I'll list a number here, and give you my reactions.

## REMARKS

| | |
|---|---|
| Never sew on a Friday or Sunday. | Sunday I believe in, but not Friday (tailors and dressmakers have to work on Fridays). |
| Never take the third light for your cigarette. | This is supposed to mean a parting. I follow this myself, but I am told that it originated in the First World War from an effort to sell more matches. |
| Never allow peacock's feathers to be brought into your house. | I do not lay much store by this. It is merely a matter of preference. |
| Never look at a new moon through glass. | As certain people under certain birth signs are affected by the different phases of the moon (you may have heard the expression "moon-struck"), I believe in this to a degree, but of course it can be argued; many people wear spectacles. |
| Never pick up a pair of scissors (or a knife) if you have dropped it yourself—always get someone else to pick it up, or it is supposed to be bad luck if you pick it up yourself, but good luck for the other person who picks it up. Tailors and dressmakers who drop their scissors, if no one else is around, will often place a | The theory here is that the sharp cutting edges of the scissors are dangerous; if they could cut your fingers, then they could cut your luck and friendship. |

foot on them first, before picking them up.

Never open an umbrella in-—This, in my opinion, is pure
doors.    fallacy; what happens in a shop where they sell umbrellas? Surely they have to test them out.

Never take May blossoms into-—Although this may be an
a room.    old-world superstition, I myself have proven this beyond coincidence to be right. It is said that sadness will descend on your home if you do this.

Never pass anyone on the-—This derives from a logical
stairs—either give way to    fact; one might accidentally
them or try to persuade them    trip the other.
to give way to you.

It is said that pearls mean-—Many people wear and look
tears.    well in pearls, and I can only think that this originated because a pearl looks, at times, like a tear. (I have heard it said that the pearl is the tear of the oyster, too.) I do not lay much store by this.

It is unlucky to burn the wood-—This I reject completely;
of the elder tree.    many people have log fires and do not know where their logs came from.

On a clear night, count seven-—It is optional, I'd say,
stars in the sky, and make a    whether you care to lay
wish.    store by this or not.

A four-leafed clover, which-—While quite beautiful, this
is very rare, is supposed to    is, of course, a freak of
bring you good fortune.    nature, and from experience I have never found this to be true.

The number thirteen is sup-—While people would often
posed to bring bad luck.    not like to put thirteen a

a table, because they know of this superstition, and would worry about the feelings of the thirteenth person, I personally do not believe this. Many of my closest friends have made a point of going out of their way to tell me that they consider thirteen to be their lucky number; if one studies numerology, thirteen represents one and three, making it four.

Always put on your right shoe first.—This originated from the fact that, as most people are right-handed, their right shoe is easier to put on.

I have given you just a few of the many thousands of superstitions that do exist, and believe me, there are thousands in many countries throughout the world. (Spain, for example, is full of superstition.) My belief is that superstitions come about in the first place when people experience either good or bad fortune after doing a certain thing, or being in a certain place or hearing a certain piece of music, say. They then associated their good or bad experience with what had preceded it, and either wanted this to happen again or, on the other hand, dreaded the recurrence of the event; therefore they told themselves that the preceding "omen" was lucky or unlucky for them.

I have never been a person to criticize unduly, I hope; there are many very highly intelligent people who do believe in some superstitions. We are all gifted with free will and free thought and are therefore entitled to our beliefs and disbeliefs; psychologically it is most important that none of us ever try to force our beliefs or feelings on others. Some people may argue that the Church itself was founded on superstitions. I will not argue for or against this. All that I can say is that in quite a few respects I myself am superstitious, so are many people I know, and I see no great harm in a few superstitions.

However, one thing I would implore of you for your own peace of mind and happiness; that is, never at any time allow these superstitions to rule your life. Accept them in a philosophical manner, have fun with them, but never allow them to worry you.

# Chapter XII

# ★ FUN—AND THE FUTURE
## —IN A TEACUP ★

This is a time-tested and long-revered method of fore-telling the future. You can have a very good time with it —and, if you allow your psychic gifts full play, you may well be able to score some direct prophetic hits.

The first thing that I must point out to you in divining the future by tea leaves is that you must allow your imagination full play, too, so that when you are concentrating on looking into the teacup at the leaves you will be able to see clearly what pictures the leaves are forming for you. I have found that in order to see the leaves most clearly one should use a cup that is completely white inside; it gives better clarity of vision for working out the future.

You first ask your sitter, when he has drunk most of his cup of tea, to take up the cup and swirl the dregs around in a circular direction from right to left, three times, thus spreading the leaves as far as possible around the inside of the cup, from the bottom to the rim. After this, he should gently drain off what liquid remains and turn the cup upside down, again very gently, resting it on the saucer in order for it to drain completely.

Now you, as the prognosticator, will pick up the cup and look into its interior. Do not be disappointed if you see very few leaves in it, for this sometimes happens; there are qualifications for this which I shall give later. Also, try not to expect the pictures which the leaves will represent to be absolutely clear in resembling what one would ex-pect to see, for, as I have said, the greater your imagination, the more you are likely to be able to discover in a cup. You must never be in too great a hurry to jump at what you think you see; when you give your reading, the logic and spontaneity, which will come with practice, are of course of the utmost importance. A point to remember is that in more cases than not one can differentiate the sex of anybody one thinks one sees in the leaves by knowing that the light leaves are invariably females and the dark leaves males; when you cannot see an actual person, but, for example, see something pertaining to a person, then you could apply a dark and light leaf principle to the coloring of the object: in other words, it will be an object belonging to a dark or fair person.

Also, it is only common sense that that which you can see extremely clearly must be more prevalent and important than the small leaf configurations which are not as clearly definable.

Regarding the past, the present and the future: that which falls to the left-hand side of the handle is usually indicative of the past tense; that which falls to the right-hand side is the present and the future, and if that which falls to the right-hand side of the cup comes rather clearly, then this is invariably very good, just as long as it is not so thick as to be indefinable. Further concerning the time element, the higher toward the brim of the cup the leaves come, the closer will be the events that you are able to forecast.

If you see your leaves following one another, almost in a semi-straight line, then these can either be routes your sitter will take or ways in which he will achieve his ends —if these appear to be quite clear, this indicates that some extremely good changes are fairly close at hand for your sitter. If either side of these routes is scattered quite a few little dots, this signifies a long life for your sitter and quite good gains moneywise.

That which you find at the bottom of your cup is, in most cases, not always happiness or good fortune and can, if not very clear, indicate that caution was needed in the past or may be needed in the future.

I shall now list the things that you are likely to be able,

with your imagination, to see in a teacup; according to how they are placed, you will know their meanings.

## An Ace

If you can see a clear ace, or an "A" such as you get in a pack of playing cards, then, if it is also with a heart, it indicates happiness to your house. If it is with a club, it indicates the afternoon or evening of the day. If it is with a diamond, it means money, and if it is with a spade, it means health.

## An Airplane

If you can clearly see an airplane in your cup, with no obstruction in its way, this is an extremely good sign, especially where your sitter's working life is concerned, and more especially if the nose of your aircraft is pointed toward the rim of the cup.

## An Anchor

The nearer to the top of the cup, the more constant and lasting is love for the sitter. At the bottom or halfway up the cup, this image indicates a successful trip taken by water.

If the anchor is erect in an upright position, then this could indicate a very happy holiday

If the anchor is not upright and appears to be held down by other leaves clouding it, then this indicates either deception or disloyalty from someone else.

If your anchor is surrounded by a few dots on either side, then this indicates that your sitter will take a voyage, but will combine business with pleasure, which should end in good results.

## An Arrow

When you can very clearly see an arrow in a cup, this indicates news, and, again, the nearer to the rim, the quicker your news will come. But it does not necessarily indicate good news if clouded. Only when it is in the clear can this be taken for pleasing communications, and, either way, if you have dots on either side of the arrow then, if it is also in the clear in its direction, this is good money news, but if it is slightly blocked in its path, then it can be taken to be money worry.

## A Bear

If you see a bear in your cup, quite naturally, as a bear is by nature fierce, this indicates that there could be slight danger in the air for your sitter; the unusual part of this symbol is the fact that, should the bear be clouded around by other leaves, then your sitter, if he is extra cautious, could avoid that danger.

There are occasions when a bear can indicate that your sitter is not going to be receiving cooperation or sympathy from those around him.

## A Bed

When you see an immaculately tidy bed, then you will know that your sitter is due for peace of mind and good fortune; but if the bed is untidy, then your sitter must take great care because he could be due for frustrations, worries and even shortage of cash.

## A Bird

It is possible to see two types of birds in a teacup. First, a small bird flying; this denotes news or chatter that the sitter will be receiving. If the flight of the bird is slightly interrupted by other tea leaves, then this news or chatter will be scandal or displeasing news. You can also see a large bird, which usually denotes news of a birth—in other words—an addition to the family of your sitter. In both these instances, if you get a letter of the alphabet near to the bird, then this will denote the initial of the direction from which the news should come.

## A Boot

It is always well, if you see a boot, to note whether it is

clearly defined or whether it is slightly broken up; if it is clearly defined, it means luck and protection from all the evils that may be around your sitter, but if slightly broken up, then it shows a risk of losses where business is concerned, or loss of prestige with people around the sitter.

If you find that the boot is near to the bottom of your cup, while this does not indicate bad luck, it does denote a slight warning that extra care is needed in what your sitter has in mind to do. If you find that the boot is three-quarters of the way up the side of the cup, or even toward the rim, then this indicates that your sitter will be able to achieve an ambition to travel. Should the toe of the boot be pointing downward, then you can take it that your sitter is likely to change either where he lives or where he works.

## A Bride

This is not a good picture to see in a teacup because it indicates sorrow and worry, and if the veil that the bride is wearing is long, then your sitter must watch out for complications and frustrations; the shorter the veil, the quicker will he be past this bother.

## A Cat

A cat is a symbol which, when seen in a cup, can be deceptive; bear in mind that cats are part of the domestic scene and therefore, if you see this animal near to the brim of your cup, then you'll know that your sitter is going to have peace of mind at home, but if, on the other hand, the cat is seen to be at the bottom or halfway up the stem of the cup, on either side, then your sitter has got to beware of slyness and deception from someone near to him. Again, if a letter of the alphabet is seen near to the cat, then that will give an indication of the initial of the person from whom your sitter has got to take care.

## A Cigar

A cigar is a warning that your sitter is being a little too extravagant, and that he needs to economize more than he is doing; as a cigar wears away with smoking, so could his material wealth.

## Clothing

If you can define from your tea leaves any article of clothing, this indicates changes for your sitter. For example, shoes usually indicate a journey, and if the shoes are very clear, this means a very successful trip.

A jacket or a jumper means that your sitter could be changing houses.

A collar and tie or a scarf denotes that your sitter will be trying for a change of job; the more clearly these are defined the more certain they are of making this change.

Headgear is of course the best symbol in this category, for it denotes great success or honors or a rise in finances.

## A Crown

This is an excellent picture to see in a teacup because it really means that your sitter will surmount most of his obstacles and come through with greater power from his experiences; should your sitter be negotiating a deal either at home or in business, the very fact that the crown is in the teacup means that he will meet with a successful conclusion for his deal.

If you see leaves in the design of a line, or lines, around or on either side of the crown, then this indicates that this person will meet with a few obstacles and delays, but with patience will still get what he desires.

## A Daisy

Whether the daisy that you see in the tea leaves is large or small does not really matter, because this is a symbol of a great deal of joy, plus quite a few admirers, so that the larger the daisy, the more popular your sitter will be.

## A Dog

When you are able to define a dog, or even just the head of a dog, in a teacup, then you will know that your sitter has got some very good friends; if you were, for example, to find one of the letters of the alphabet near to this symbol of a dog, then you would be able to give the initial of that friend to your sitter.

Here it is the position of the dog that is of great importance when giving a reading. For example, if the dog should appear to be making his way to the rim of the cup, then it means that your sitter can expect some very good news from a genuine friend.

If, on the other hand, you find a lot of other leaves impeding or surrounding the dog, this could indicate that someone else is trying to create a quarrel between the two of them, and that deception is close at hand from this other person. If, on the other hand, you find that the picture of the dog is toward the bottom of the cup, then this will mean that your sitter has a friend who is going to be in need of his help.

## An Egg

If you see an egg very clearly defined, this means either that your sitter is going to make an excellent change for himself, or that he is going to try out a new way of life. If the egg appears to be either slightly cracked or even broken, it can either mean the news of a birth or that a new project your sitter may have in mind would be better delayed for the time being. (Here, of course you must use your imagination according to the other surrounding leaves.)

## A Feather

This is a sign which in effect is a slight warning to your sitter that he must, for the time being, work harder. It is obvious if you see a feather in the cup that your sitter has been relaxing too much and not putting his best foot forward in his business or home life.

## A Fish

This is one of the best objects to see in a teacup because

it is extremely fortunate; as fishes swim quite fast, so should the luck of your sitter become better and better.

## A Hand

If the hand that you see is either bent or held like a fist, then it means that your sitter is not giving of his best where his ambitions are concerned, and must do so; otherwise he could meet with failure. On the other hand, should the hand be very clear and open, then it means that quite a lot of help and cooperation and good friendship are coming the way of your sitter.

## A Heart

For a single unattached person to have a heart in his teacup indicates either an engagement or a marriage in the near future. For a married person to have a heart in his cup, the signs are for great and genuine future affection being his.

If one should see a lot of dots around the heart in the cup, this means that he will be blessed with financial success as well as affection and loyalty. If you can see a letter of the alphabet near to the heart, this signifies the initial of the person who stands so genuinely in love with your sitter.

## A Horse

A horse is the symbol of emotion, and romantic emotion at that—in other words, someone who genuinely loves your sitter. If the horse appears to be running, this means news from a loved one which should please your sitter. If, however, the horse's progress appears to be impeded by clusters of tea leaves, this would indicate that the person who loves your sitter either has a relative complex or has a tie that he must surmount before true and lasting happiness can bring him permanently together with your sitter.

Should there be anywhere around your horse a little circle or a three-quarter completed circle of leaves—even dots—then, if your sitter is single, this would indicate that she is going to be proposed to in the very near future.

If there are quite a few dots all around any part of the horse, this usually indicates a financially comfortable lover for your sitter.

## A Horseshoe

This is another excellent symbol for your sitter, especially if it is the right way up (open part up), holding the luck in. If the horseshoe is on its side, or if the points are downward, this indicates that while your sitter will still be lucky, he may have a few problems that he will have to overcome first.

## A House

To see a house, whether clear or not, in a teacup means security and independence for your sitter, plus a lot of happiness; the bigger the house, the greater should be your sitter's safety.

## A Ladder

A ladder is usually seen in an ambitious person's teacup; it shows the advancement he is likely to make through life. If it is a long ladder, then he is likely to grasp a very good opportunity in the near future. If a very short ladder, then it means that he will do very well through a series of small opportunities.

## A Leg

A leg, of course, denotes progress, especially if it appears to be striding. If seen very clearly, it also tells you that your sitter has an almost psychic understanding of those around him, and the people that he meets.

## A Moon

If you see just a quarter moon, you should know that your sitter has it in mind to try out something new. If the moon is complete, then your sitter is surely involved in a pleasing romance with someone who is genuine; if single, your sitter is likely to marry this person. Should you see clouds around the moon, then this indicates that your sitter must not build too much on the romance, for if he does so he could meet with later regrets.

## A Pyramid

This usually represents a skeleton in someone's cupboard —in other words, a secret that may have been causing worry. But the fact that the pyramid itself has been revealed in the cup of your sitter indicates that he is coming out of this dark shadow into good fortune.

## A Ring

This depicts an event of some importance about to happen in or around the life of your sitter; just what it may be you will be able to determine by what is near the ring in your teacup. For example, if an anchor is near it, this means that an engagement will be announced, which should lead on to a happy marriage.

If a heart is near it, and both the ring and the heart are near the rim of the cup, then it means a speedy marriage.

The deeper down in the base of the cup the ring is seen, the longer will be the engagement before the marriage. Should you see a few clouds around the ring, and, just on the right-hand side of the handle, a cross near to it, this will indicate that the person will become engaged, but that the engagement will be broken.

## A Ship

If you see a ship in your cup, which is not particularly clear and has little dots all around it, this indicates that your sitter is in need of good advice from a genuinely concerned person. Should your ship have sails, and should one of these appear to be torn, then your sitter needs to be cautious, for it means that someone intends to do him harm. When you see a very clear outline of a ship, and the path in front of it is clear, too, this means excellent fortune for your sitter.

## A Snake

This is very indicative of enemies; the nearer to the top of the cup it comes, the more chance your sitter has of escaping his enemies. If, however, the snake is at the bottom, your sitter would do well to sit on the fence and do nothing for the time being.

If you should see a letter of the alphabet near to this snake, that should give you an indication of the initial of the enemy.

## A Star

If you see a star, halfway between the bottom and the rim, and this star is clear, then your sitter can expect some very good luck and excellent opportunities in the near future. If a star is toward the bottom of the cup, then this could be a slight warning of dangers or little accidents. When you have more than one star, this usually means that your sitter's home life should be blessed with a happy family and several children.

## A Tree

Trees in effect are wishes; the more trees you are able to see in the cup, the greater is the chance of your sitter's wishes being granted. If you see a single solid tree, this means very good health plus comfort.

## A Wheel

When you see a wheel toward the rim of the cup, this means that your sitter can expect some very quick success or even a win or an inheritance. If you see a wheel which has what looks like a small block in its path that could stop its free motion, then this can be taken as a warning that your sitter must take more care and give more concentration to the important things around him.

Should you pick up a teacup in which you see very few leaves at all, those leaves you do see will, in nine cases out of ten, be more clear in their definition; this will mean that there is nothing impeding progress, and it can be taken as a good sign. If, on the other hand, the leaves make no sense to you whatsoever, then it would be wise to ask your sitter to try again at a later time. When you have tried to study a teacup without interruption, and on your own, concentrating well, you should find that after a short while you *will be* able to see things; as long as you are sensible in your interpretations, you should derive not only satisfaction but a lot of fun from this method of foretelling the future.